Clergy Tax

DAVID EPSTEIN
TAX ATTORNEY

Regal

A Division of Gospel Light
Ventura, California, U.S.A.

Published by Regal Books
A Division of Gospel Light
Ventura, California, U.S.A.
Printed in U.S.A.

Regal Books is a ministry of Gospel Light, an evangelical Christian publisher dedicated to serving the local church. We believe God's vision for Gospel Light is to provide church leaders with biblical, user-friendly materials that will help them evangelize, disciple and minister to children, youth and families.

It is our prayer that this Regal book will help you discover biblical truth for your own life and help you meet the needs of others. May God richly bless you.

For a free catalog of resources from Regal Books/Gospel Light please contact your Christian supplier or call 1-800-4-GOSPEL.

Cover Design by Barbara LeVan Fisher
Interior Design by Britt Rocchio
Edited by Pam Weston and Patti Pennington Virtue

ISBN 0-8307-2470-2
© 1999 by David Epstein, J.D.
All rights reserved.
Printed in U.S.A.

Read the Following Limited Warranty Information Before Using This Product:

Contents

Letter to the Pastor

We know you hate taxes! (Who doesn't?) That's why we wrote this program, to help take this burden off you. That's why, to prepare your tax return this year:

You only have to find the numbers that go into **12 Boxes**.

The idea behind *ClergyTax*® is to "paint-by-number." And:

You only need about 12 numbers to fill out your tax return.

ClergyTax® takes you step-by-step, and tells you what each of the 12 numbers is, and shows you exactly how to find each number. The worksheets make it easy.

Most of the 12 numbers are already at your fingertips, in the "tax documents" you get at the end of the year. But it's fair to tell you that a few of them are hard to find, and one in particular is going to be hard for those ministers who don't keep good records: the amount you spent for housing allowance.

The better your records are organized, the easier time you're going to have preparing your tax return each year. If you have good records, *ClergyTax*® will make it all easy. Even if you don't have good records, *ClergyTax*® will point the way for you, and help make collecting the information you need more painless, and show you exactly where to put it.

Basically all you have to do is:

find the 12 numbers, plug them into your tax return.

Then you're done!

This year, in particular, it's going to be much more important to have a correct minister's tax return than in the past.

That's because some of the most sweeping changes in the past 30 years have been made to the tax code, and major changes now affect ministers directly.

Here's how *ClergyTax*® helps you stay in line with the new laws:

- Helps you have a stealth tax return—the more you follow the directions in *ClergyTax*®, the lower your "audit profile";
- Helps you avoid red flags and have a tax return that's nearly invisible to the IRS
- Helps point you toward the lowest tax position for a minister in your particular financial situation
- Updated each year to reflect the latest tax law changes
- Contains appendices with a quick review of new laws every church and minister should be aware of!

One final thought: The rules in *ClergyTax*® have been checked by the tax authorities in the IRS national office, as well as key IRS-exempt organizations' specialists in other parts of the country, and they did not find anything in the *ClergyTax*® rules they disagreed with (actually, they did find one or two things initially, but we made the changes they recommended). We have also had the rules you read here checked by many other tough critics to see if we could improve in any areas.

Our hope is that eventually IRS agents will know that ministers who use *ClergyTax*® are not worth auditing anyway because their returns meet all the required standards. We believe *ClergyTax*® is the wave of the future.

How This Book Is Organized

Now, we're ready to begin. Here's how *ClergyTax*® is organized: First complete the **12 Boxes** most ministers need to complete their tax returns. Worksheets guide you to filling out many of the boxes.

After you complete this section, you're probably 90 percent to 100 percent done with your tax return, unless you have a lot of complicated issues. All you need to do after you complete this section is scan down the checklist for Part 2, and see if any of the items apply to you. If so, complete the items that apply to you, and then you're done!

If you're truly a "tax junkie," you can continue on to the appendices, where we have included helpful hints for checking your return and lowering your tax liability. The appendices give all sorts of helpful information about various aspects of ministers' income taxes. You don't need to read any appendix to fill out your tax return (unless you get a 1099 from your church). Those parts are available for when you have trouble falling asleep at night, and for those few pastors who like to play Certified Public Accountant (both of you).

Great Idea

After you have placed the necessary information in the **12 Boxes** on your tax forms (as illustrated on the sample tax forms), instead of trying to do all the math calculations yourself, just plug in the 12 numbers you've filled in to a tax software program and it will do all the math for you. Many ministers now use *ClergyTax*® as a companion guide when doing their taxes by computer. The forms in this book are keyed right to where the numbers go in most tax preparation software programs.

General Information

The following will help you assemble some of the tax information that will be convenient to have at your fingertips when you are doing your tax return. Having this information ready ahead of time should make filling out your return much quicker and easier.

Tips

It is important that the information you use to prepare your tax return for 1999 is true and complete to the best of your knowledge and belief. On the other hand, if information is missing or destroyed that is needed to complete your return, simply do your best and make the best good faith estimate you can. When making an estimate, keep notes about how you arrived at the estimate so you can remember later if necessary.

Always keep the notes and papers you used to prepare your tax return. Keep these papers as long as you keep your tax return itself. It is better to make a photocopy of your return so you have an exact copy, rather than the common practice of just keeping a "penciled in" handwritten version.

If you have a refund due this year, the IRS will send you the refund, unless you enter the amount of your refund on Form 1040, line 61, to apply your refund to your tax for next year.

Did you file an income tax return last year?

❑ yes ❑ no

If yes, please have handy a copy of your 1998 federal and state tax returns for reference.

If no, you may need to consult a competent tax professional **immediately**.

Did your church keep a payroll sheet for you in 1999?

❑ yes ❑ no

If yes, please have a copy of it nearby when you do your return.

If no, they could start this year, because this is an easy way for you to have most of the numbers you need right at your fingertips when you fill out your return.

You'll need all W-2s, 1099s, 1098s (for your mortgage interest and taxes) you've received during the year. It's a good idea to start a file at the beginning of each year, and put all your tax-related papers in it as they come in. Then you'll have everything ready to sit down and knock out your tax return.

Use the new knowledge you have gained from using this year's edition of *ClergyTax*® to begin your tax planning for 2000. You have the rest of the year for the *ClergyTax*® system to help you analyze your tax situation and point out ways to lower your tax and to keep a lower audit profile.

In your church, for example, you may want to do a complete salary restructuring, or completely revamp the accounting system.

Part 1
The 12 Boxes You Need
to Fill Out Your Tax Return

Each of the 12 Boxes is numbered—you guessed it—1 through 12.

A section of sample forms is also included. These sample forms are a W-2 and a tax return (1040, Schedule A, Form 2106, Schedule B, Schedule C and Schedule SE).

The sample forms are keyed to the 12 Boxes.

For example, once you have the number for Box 1, all you have to do is go to the sample forms to see where to put that number.

It's paint-by-number easy.

Start with a Correct W-2

First, to have a correct tax return, you must have a correct W-2. If your W-2 is wrong, then your tax return will be wrong, too—and that could lead to big surprises if you're audited.

(If you still want to have a 1099 after reading the first part of the 1099 section of this book, then follow the directions in the last part of that same 1099 section.)

To have a correct W-2, just use the simple worksheet that follows. Plug in the numbers, add them up and you should have the right W-2 for a minister.

This section walks you through the steps to get the right W-2 in the first place. It's a good idea to go through the worksheet, and then compare the results to the W-2 you actually got from your church. If the two match—great! If not, use the numbers from the worksheet on your tax return. (You may want your accountant to file a corrected W-2 for you—or get Form W-2c from the IRS.)

You can use these numbers on your tax return, even if your church did not give you a W-2.

W-2 Income Worksheet

Box 1

Box 1

Find line 1 on your W-2. If you don't have a W-2, just look at the sample W-2 in the sample forms section of this book.

This W-2 income worksheet is how you determine what number goes in line 1 of your W-2. The number for Box 1 is the amount that should be in line 1 of your W-2 form. Correct W-2 income is the number from Box 1.

The number from Box 1 also goes on line 7 of your tax return, Form 1040, page 1.

(Look at the sample forms section, and you will see that each of the 12 Boxes is keyed to the line of the tax form where it belongs. Some of the 12 Boxes are used in more than one place.)

Here is what always goes in Box 1, that is, these items should have been included on your W-2 in line 1. To find out the number that goes in Box 1, add up the amounts below, and put them in Box 1:

1.   The regular salary(s) you receive from your church (not including your housing allowance).

     Write the amount here: $ _____.

2.   Christmas bonuses, even if it was collected as a "love offering."

     Write the amount here: $ _____.

3.   Year-end and birthday bonuses, even if they were collected as "love offerings."

     Write the amount here: $ _____.

4.   If you own your car, auto allowance paid in cash or by check (for which no mileage was submitted; if you were paid 31 cents a mile by the church for miles you drove on church business, then you don't have to put this money in Box 1).

     Write the amount here: $ _____.

5.   If the church owns your car, personal use of the church auto (use the Annual Lease Value Worksheet).

     Write the amount here: $ _____.

6.   All life insurance premiums paid by the church (except [1] premiums for group term insurance up to $50,000 face amount; and [2] policies from which the church gets the money after your lifetime).

     Write the amount here: $ _____.

7.   Travel allowances, clothing allowances and housecleaning allowances—these are all taxable items, even if they are listed as part of the "housing allowance."

     Write the amount here: $ _____.

8.   Vacations paid for by the church—you did not perform ministry, but just "took some time off."

     Write the amount here: $ _____.

9. School tuition paid by your church for your children—if your children attend a school that is not related to your church (see the reference section in Part 2 for information about some types of church-paid school tuitions that may not be taxable).

Write the amount here: $ _____.

10. Social Security tax paid by the church for you as a minister on top of regular salary. This is not the same as tax withheld from a minister's salary; this is tax that is paid on behalf of a minister so the minister won't have to pay it.

Write the amount here: $ _____.

11. Federal or state income tax paid by the church for you as a minister on top of regular salary; this is not the same as tax withheld from a minister's salary; this is tax that is paid on behalf of a minister so the minister won't have to pay it.

Write the amount here: $ _____.

12. Pay advances, even if they were called "loans."

Write the amount here: $ _____.

13. Expenses reimbursed under a nonaccountable plan. If your church does not have an accountable reimbursement plan (sample minutes are included in appendix 7), any amounts the church reimburses you for business expenses are taxable, and must be reported. (You may still be able to deduct these expenses—see Deductions.) You can avoid this problem altogether by simply having a church board meeting and adopting the sample reimbursement minutes we have included in this manual.

Write the amount here: $ _____.

14. Excess housing allowance: Add up how much you spent on housing items (use the worksheet showing a list of housing items you can use). Subtract what you spent on housing items from the amount the church paid you for housing allowance. If the church paid you more for housing than you actually spent on housing items, the excess goes in Box 1. (Use the number from the Excess Housing worksheet: HOUSING ➡ Box 4.)

Write the amount here: $ _____.

15. Add up all the lines from the previous items and put the total here:

This is Box 1 $ _____.

What to do with the number in Box 1:

First, compare the number in Box 1 to the number in line 1 of your W-2. Do they match?

If they match, great! If not, don't use your W-2 to fill out your tax return. Instead, use the number you just totaled for Box 1.

Now, take the number for Box 1 and put it on line 7 of your Form 1040, page 1. See the sample forms section for an illustration of where the number in Box 1 goes.

➡ Don't forget to carry the number from *line 2* of your W-2 to *line 57* of your Form 1040, page 2.

(State income tax from lines 18 and 21 of your W-2 goes on your state income tax return, if any, and also on Schedule A, line 5 of your federal return.)

If Box 1 plus your housing allowance is less than about $26,000 to $30,000, depending on the number of children you have, you may qualify for the Earned Income Credit, a type of extra refund from the IRS. To find out, fill out Schedule EIC (See IRS instructions).

➡ If you didn't get a W-2, see Part 2, item 1 for what to do. You'll also need to use the number from the Box 1 worksheet.

➡ If you received a 1099, see appendix 2 for what to do. You'll also need to use the Box 1 worksheet.

Now: What happens if you have a number on one of the previous lines—but it was left off your W-2c (Can you spell S-I-B-E-R-I-A?) Seriously, all you have to do is pick option 1 or option 2:

Option 1: On your tax return, use the correct number you calculated for Box 1. Then file form W-2c to correct your W-2.

-or-

Option 2: Use the W-2 your church gave you, even though it is incorrect. Then enter the items that were left off your W-2 on line 21 of your tax return, Form 1040, page 1. (If you are not Social Security tax exempt, you'll have to carry the amount on line 21 to line 2 of your Schedule SE.) Attach a note to your return showing how you arrived at the number you put on line 21. A sample form to help you do this follows. Write in the description of the income, and then fill in the amount. You can use the worksheet—just make a copy, complete it and attach it to your tax return. After entering the total on line 21, add the notation: "see attached schedule."

Supporting Schedule to Form 1040, Line 21

Name of Minister: _____

Social Security Number: _____ - _____ - _____

Note: The following items were not included on the W-2 issued by the church.

Excess housing allowance	$
Christmas/year-end/birthday bonus	$
Personal use of church auto	$
Love offering	$
Pay advance(s)	$
Cash auto allowance	$
Clothing allowance	$
Housecleaning allowance	$
Life insurance premiums paid by church	$
Social Security tax paid by church	$
Federal or state income tax paid by church	$
Personal vacation paid by church	$
School tuition paid for pastor's children by church at nonchurch school	$
Expenses reimbursed under nonaccountable plan	$
Other:	$
TOTAL:	$

Other Income Items and Where They Go

Box 2

Box 2

For Your Spouse's Church Salary, or for Income Earned Outside the Church

A. What was your spouse's church salary in 1999? $_____ (not including housing) If your spouse received a W-2, add the number from line 1 of her W-2 to line 7 of your Form 1040, page 1. Add the number from line 2 of her W-2 to line 57 of page 2 of Form 1040. And add the number(s), if any, from lines 18 and 21 of her W-2 to Schedule A, line 5 of your tax return.

B. Did you work anywhere else besides the church in 1999?

❑ yes ❑ no

If you did, and you received a W-2, add the number from line 1 of this W-2 to line 7 of your Form 1040, page 1. Add the number from line 2 of this W-2 to line 57 of page 2 of Form 1040. And add the number(s), if any, from lines 18 and 21 of this W-2 to Schedule A, line 5 of your tax return.

If you did, and you received a 1099, add it to line 21 on page 1 of Form 1040. Use the "Other" line of the line 21 worksheet for the total of your 1099 income from outside the church. (*Alternative*: You can enter this income on Schedule C, line 1 instead, but doing so will increase your chances of an audit.)

C. Did your spouse work anywhere else besides the church in 1999?

❑ yes ❑ no

If your spouse received a salary or other kinds of income from somewhere besides the church:

If your spouse received a W-2, add the number from line 1 of her W-2 to line 7 of your Form 1040, page 1. Add the number from line 2 of her W-2 to line 57 of page 2 of Form 1040. And add the number(s), if any, from lines 18 and 21 of her W-2 to Schedule A, line 5 of your tax return.

If your spouse received a 1099, add it to line 21 on page 1 of Form 1040. Use the "Other" line of the line 21 worksheet for the total of her 1099 income from outside the church. (*Alternative*: You can enter this income on Schedule C, line 1 instead, but doing so will increase your chances of an audit.)

Note: If you or your spouse received a 1099 *from your church* for work you did during 1998, you need to go to appendix 2, How to Handle 1099s. That's because if the church is your main source of income, 1099s should be entered on Schedule C, line 1. Appendix 2, How to Handle 1099s, tells you how to do this.

Note: Some tax practitioners think it is correct to report 1099 income on line 21 of Form 1040. Others will tell you it has to go on Schedule C (which is more prone to being audited). In some cases, *where* the income is reported can cause a "matching inquiry." This is merely a letter from the IRS because it can't figure out where you reported a certain amount of income. These letters can be answered by mail.

Here is my position about where to report income on your tax return: As long as the income is reported correctly regarding amount, and as long as the correct tax is paid (income tax as well as Social Security tax, if it is due), it has been my experience that the IRS really doesn't care if you dotted every *i* and crossed every *t*. On Schedule C particularly, the IRS will often take the position with ministers that you can't use it anyway, even if the income you received was reported on a 1099.

The big advantage to a Schedule C is that when you take expenses on that form, they count as deductions against both income as well as Social Security (or self-employment) taxes. The IRS doesn't like this, and will often try to move that income somewhere else on your return so it can move the expenses to Schedule A, which gives the government an advantage.

Note: You can still deduct your church-related business expenses from Schedule SE income even if you use line 21 (see later in this manual for instructions at Box 6 for how to do this).

Bottom line: If you report 1099 income on line 21 of your 1040, the IRS isn't likely to care, and you get the plus of a return that has a lower audit profile

Box 3

Box 3

Use this Box if you received a W-2 from your church, but also had either of the following kinds of outside income:

A. Honorariums from outside speaking $ _____
➡ But note: If these items went directly to the church, instead of to you, they are not income and don't have to be reported.

B. Fees paid directly to you from parishioners for weddings, funerals, baptisms and masses
                                                         $ _____
➡ But note: If these items went directly to the church, instead of to you, they are not income and don't have to be reported.

Enter either of these items on line 21 of Form 1040. Write in the description of the income, and then fill in the amount. If you are not Social Security tax exempt, also enter this income on Schedule SE, line 2.

Don't carry this income to Schedule SE if you have filed Form 4361 to be exempt from Social Security tax.

Box 4

Box 4

Interest (you'll need the Form 1099 you received from each bank or company that paid you interest)

Name of Bank or Company	Amount
_____	$ _____
_____	$ _____
_____	$ _____

Enter these amounts on line 1 of Schedule B of your tax return. If the total is less than $400, you can just enter the total on line 8a of your Form 1040, page 1.

Note: Be sure to check the appropriate box(es) under items 11 and 12 of Part III of Schedule B if you had more than $400 of interest for 1999.

Box 5

Box 5

Dividends (you'll need the Form 1099 you received from each company that paid you dividends)

Name of Bank or Company   Amount

_____ $ _____

_____ $ _____

_____ $ _____

Enter these amounts on line 5 of Schedule B of your tax return. If the total is less than $400, you can just enter the total on line 9 of your Form 1040, page 1. Note: Be sure to check the appropriate box(es) under items 11 and 12 of Part III of Schedule B if you had more than $400 of dividends for 1999.

Box 6

Box 6

Figuring Self-Employment (Social Security) Tax for Ministers
Unless you are exempt from Social Security tax because you've filed Form 4361, you have to pay Social Security (self-employment) tax on your earnings as a minister. This tax applies both to your salary, honorariums, other earned income *and* to your housing allowance.

Salary
On Schedule SE, enter your church salary (this is the number from Box 1) on line 5a. (It is also correct to report this income on line 2 of Schedule SE instead.)

Note: *Do not* enter your salary on Schedule SE if you have filed Form 4361 and are exempt from paying Social Security (self-employment) tax.

Line 21 Items
If you have entered items on line 21, Form 1040, page 1, and if you are not Social Security tax exempt, carry the total of the items on line 21 to line 2 of Schedule SE.

Note: Remember to subtract the total expenses on your Minister's Professional Expenses Worksheet (Box 7) from your line 21 items before entering them on line 2. (You can also do this by entering your line 21 items on line 2 of Schedule SE, and then entering Box 7 as a *negative number* on line 1 of Schedule SE—write "minister's expenses" on the dotted line to the left.)

Note: I guess every year *ClergyTax*® is published, I am going to get letters about how I have "tortured" the IRS forms to meet the needs of ministers. For example, your accountant is going to tell you that from the beginning of the world until now, no one has ever entered a minister's business expenses as a negative number on Line A-3 of the Schedule SE worksheet. So why should all that change now? Here's why: I have spent hours on the phone to the Forms Section at the IRS National Office in Washington, D.C., asking them to add an extra line to Schedule SE for ministers. This extra line is needed so ministers can deduct their church business expenses against their self-employment income, such as their salary and housing allowance. The IRS instructions show that a minister's business expenses are a legitimate deduction on Schedule SE, but there is no line on Schedule SE to list these expenses. Traditionally, ministers have had to deduct their expenses before

Box 6

they wrote the income on Schedule SE. This causes many ministers to overlook and miss out on this legitimate deduction. To me, it is much easier to show the expenses on Line A-3 as a negative number, so that it's netted from your housing allowance and your church salary. You'll get the same result as the other method, and it's much more clearly laid out (plus hopefully you won't forget anything). If the IRS won't add a line to accommodate ministers (they say there are too many lines on this form already!), then I don't see why the form can't be "tortured" to fit the needs of ministers.

Note: *Do not* carry over to Schedule SE the amount(s) on line 21 if you have filed Form 4361 and are exempt from paying Social Security (self-employment) tax.

Note: If you are a minister, and line 4 of your W-2 shows Social Security withheld, then your W-2 is incorrect and must be amended.

Housing Allowance

If you are *not* Social Security tax exempt, then on Schedule SE (long form), enter your housing allowance on line 2.

Note: Remember to subtract the total expenses on your Minister's Professional Expenses Worksheet (Box 7) from your housing before entering it on line 2. (You can also do this by entering your housing allowance on line 2 of Schedule SE, and then entering Box 7 as a *negative number* on line 1 of Schedule SE—write "minister's expenses" on the dotted line to the left.)

Note: *Do not* enter your housing allowance on Schedule SE if you have filed Form 4361 and are exempt from paying Social Security (self-employment) tax.

Parsonage

Does the church own and provide a parsonage for you?

❏ yes ❏ no

If yes, then on Schedule SE (long form), enter on line 2 the rental value of the parsonage, plus rental value of furnishings, plus utilities.

Note: Remember to subtract the expenses on your Minister's Professional Expenses Worksheet (Box 7) from your parsonage amount before entering it on line 2. (You can also do this by entering your parsonage expenses on line 2 of Schedule SE, and then entering Box 7 as a *negative number* on line 1 of Schedule SE—write "minister's expenses" on the dotted line to the left.)

To find the rental value of your parsonage, fill in this blank: About how much would the parsonage rent for if the church rented it out instead of letting you live there? $ _____/month. (Consider factors such as church use of the parsonage, number of ministers occupying the parsonage, no choice in matter of parsonage assigned and so on.)

NOTE: If you are retired and your church designates your housing allowance from your pension, then it should not be subject to Social Security (self-employment) tax on Schedule SE. This is so even though the new Ministers' Audit Guidelines released by the IRS say that a retired minister's housing allowance is subject to SE tax. I and other tax commentators thought that this was an incorrect position in the IRS Ministers' Audit Guidelines, and we believed it would be corrected. Congress acted during 1996, and passed a law that now says retired ministers may now receive a housing allowance, and owe no Social Security tax on it. Utilities are also covered. (This benefit is retroactive, and retired ministers who paid Social Security tax on their housing allowances in 1995, 1996 or 1997 can file amended returns to claim a refund.)

Box 6

Box 6—Epstein Method

Worksheet to Figure Minister's Self-Employment (Social Security) Tax

Salary	$ _____	(goes on line 5a of Schedule SE)
Line 21 Income Items	$ _____	(goes on line 2 of Schedule SE)
Schedule C Income	$ _____	(goes on line 2 of Schedule SE)
Housing Allowance	$ _____	(goes on line 2 of Schedule SE)
Fair Value of Parsonage	$ _____	(goes on line 2 of Schedule SE)
Subtotal:	$ _____	

Less: Total amount of all church-related business expenses paid out of minister's own pocket, and not reimbursed by church (Box 7):

– $ _____

(goes on line 1 of Schedule SE as a *negative number*)

Subtotal:

$ _____

× .9235 (multiply this subtotal by .9235)

Total: $ _____ This is Box 6

This total should be the same as line 6 of Schedule SE.
This is the amount that is subject to tax on Schedule SE.

Box 6—Traditional Method

Worksheet to Figure Minister's Self-Employment (Social Security) Tax

Salary	$ _____
Line 21 Income Items	$ _____
Schedule C Income	$ _____
Housing Allowance	$ _____
Fair Value of Parsonage	$ _____
Subtotal:	$ _____
Less:	

Total amount of all church-related business expenses paid out of minister's own pocket, and not reimbursed by church (Box 7):

– $ _____

Total: $ _____

This total should be entered on line 2 of Schedule SE.
Attach this worksheet to your tax return.

Instead of entering each of these items separately, you can simply enter the bottom line total of Box 6 on Schedule SE, line 6 and then attach this worksheet to your tax return to show how you arrived at this number.

So you have 3 options:

1. Either put Box 6 on line 6 of Schedule SE, and attach this worksheet to show how you got the number; or
2. Put your church salary on line 5a of Schedule SE; put your line 21 items, your Schedule C net income and your housing/parsonage expenses on line 2 of Schedule SE; put Box 7 as a *negative number* on line 1 of Schedule SE; or
3. Use the traditional method worksheet, and put the total from it on line 2 of your Schedule SE.

Note: Whether you use Option 1, Option 2 or Option 3, you should have arrived at the same number on *line 6 of Schedule SE.*

Note: *The Deason rule does not apply on Schedule SE.* So do *not* reduce your business expenses by the percentage of your housing allowance. Subtract the full amount of your church-related business expenses on this worksheet.

1999 Housing Allowance

Home Owned or Rented/Housing Allowance Received

- How to figure your correct housing allowance.
- How to figure "excess housing allowance."

You will need the following information to figure the amount of your housing allowance. Several worksheets follow that will help you find these numbers.

You may find this section a little frustrating because although the housing allowance is one of the best tax benefits available to ministers, it is also one of the most confusing to figure. So plan on putting a little effort into this section, but in return you may reap big rewards at tax time.

The housing allowance is limited to the least of:

1. Amount designated as housing allowance.
   Housing ➡ Box 1
2. Amount actually spent on housing expenses.
   Housing ➡ Box 2
3. Fair rental value or FRV.
   Housing ➡ Box 3

Now, use the next three worksheets to figure these items.

Housing ➡ Box 1

How much housing allowance did the church designate for you in 1999 in addition to your regular salary?
$_____ [A]

Has your housing amount been designated in your church minute book?
❑ yes   ❑ no

If no: You need to be sure you have church minutes for all housing in advance of when the housing is paid out to any ministers.

Was your housing money actually paid to you (or was it at least paid by the church directly for housing items on your behalf)?
❑ yes   ❑ no

If no: If the amount of housing money you actually got was different from what was designated for you, please put the actual amount paid to you here:
$_____ [B]

(please include any money paid by the church directly for housing items on your behalf).

Look at lines [A] and [B]—which is less? Put that amount here: $_____

This number is Housing ➡ Box 1

Housing ➡ Box 2

This is the most complete listing of allowable housing expenses we know of. It was compiled from Letter Rulings, tax court cases and actual audits. Please enter the amount of 1999 housing (or parsonage) expenses you paid in column 1. (If your church paid any of these for you, please enter the amount in column 2.)

Item	Column 1 Paid by You	Column 2 Paid by Church
Rent	$	$
Mortgage payments	$	$
Down payment	$	$
Insurance on home and contents	$	$
Real estate taxes	$	$
Maintenance, pest control, etc.	$	$
Repairs, plumbing, electric work, etc.	$	$
Kitchen items, plates, silverware, dishes, utensils, cups, glasses, cookware, etc.	$	$
Household cleaning supplies, soap, detergent, tissue, brooms, light bulbs, trash bags, etc.	$	$
Furniture and furnishings— purchase, repair and upkeep	$	$
Appliances—purchase, repair and upkeep	$	$
Curtains, rugs, linens, towels, pictures, frames, decorating items, wallpaper, door locks, etc.	$	$
Utilities (electricity, gas, telephone, sewer, water, trash pickup, cable TV, firewood)	$	$
Landscaping, lawn services, gardening, fencing	$	$
Adding on rooms or other structural changes	$	$
Other: (but not food or servants or entertainment)	$	$
Totals:	$	$

Housing ➡ Box 3

How to Estimate the Fair Rental Value of Your Home (FRV)

How much do you think your home would sell for if you sold it today? $ _____

Multiply this number by .01 $ _____ [A]

(Example: Your home is worth $100,000. So multiply $100,000 by .01, and that equals $1,000).

Please note: Where church-related meetings are conducted in a parsonage, more than one minister living in the same parsonage, no choice in matter of the parsonage assigned or similar factors, the fair rental value of the parsonage may be considerably less than the value arrived at by this formula.

How much did you pay for your furniture? $ _____
Multiply this number by 2, then divide by 24 $ _____ [B]

(Example: Your furniture cost $9,000. So $9,000 times 2 equals $18,000. Then $18,000 divided by 24 equals $750.)

Estimate your total utility bill each month. Be sure to include electricity, gas, telephone, sewer, water, trash pickup, cable TV, firewood, etc.

$_____ [C]

Now, add up [A], [B] and [C]:

$ _____ .
This number is: Housing ➡ Box 3

This is an estimate of the maximum amount of housing allowance you qualify for each month. The IRS calls this number the "FRV."

Excess Housing Allowance Worksheet
Housing ➡ Box 4

(Carry this number to the last item on the Box 1 worksheet.)

A. Was any of the housing allowance you received not actually spent on housing items?

❏ yes   ❏ no

If no, *stop here,* you don't have an excess housing allowance.

If yes, how much was not spent on housing?
This amount goes on line 21 of Form 1040, page 1.
Write "excess housing allowance" on the line.

$ _____

Hint: Here's how to figure how much of your housing allowance was not actually spent:

Enter the number from Housing ➡ Box 1, [B] worksheet here:

$_____ [A]

(This is the amount the church actually gave you for housing.)

Enter the number from the Housing ➡ Box 2 worksheet here:

$_____ [B]

(This is the amount you actually spent on housing; use total from column 1 only.)

Compare these two numbers. Is [A] more than [B]?
If yes, then you have excess housing allowance.
How much is the excess housing amount?

B. Subtract [B] from [A] and enter the result here:

$ _____

This is the excess amount that goes on line 21 according to the directions for Box 1 above.

Example: If [A], the housing allowance the church paid you, is $20,000; and [B], the amount you actually spent on housing, is $15,000; then you just subtract [B] ($15,000) from [A] ($20,000), and you get the excess amount of $5,000, which goes on line 21 according to the directions for Box 1 above.

Note: The entire amount of housing allowance paid to you is subject to self-employment (Social Security) tax unless you are exempt from Social Security tax because you have filed Form 4361, or are retired.

Note: If you are retired and your church designates your housing allowance from your pension, then it should not be subject to Social Security (self-employment) tax on Schedule SE. This is so even though the new Ministers' Audit Guidelines released by the IRS say that a retired minister's housing allowance *is* subject to SE tax. I, and other tax commentators, thought that this was an incorrect position in the IRS Ministers' Audit Guidelines, and we believed it would be corrected. Congress acted during 1996, and passed a law that now says that retired ministers may now receive a housing allowance, and owe no Social Security tax on it. Utilities are also covered. (This benefit is retroactive, and retired ministers who paid Social Security tax on their housing allowances in 1996, 1997 or 1998 can file amended returns to claim a refund. Note: 1996 returns should be amended no later than April 15, 2000 or three years from the filing date, whichever is sooner.)

Deductions

Box 7

Box 7

Minister's Professional Expense Worksheet

Did the church reimburse you for church-related expenses in 1999?   ❏ yes   ❏ no

If no, fill out Box 7, the Minister's Professional Expense Worksheet.

If yes, has your church adopted an accountable church reimbursement policy in the minutes?

❏ yes   ❏ no

If yes, fill out Box 7 *only for expenses for which your church has not reimbursed you.*

If no, you are in big trouble (see the next to last item under Box 1.)

(Also see appendix 7 for Sample Minutes.)

List expenses on the Minister's Professional Expense Worksheet you paid for *out of your own pocket*, and for which you were *never reimbursed* by the church. (This includes seminars, conventions and so forth. This page is for items not paid for by the church. It is best to keep a trip diary for your records to show the ministry purpose of travel.)

List the total of your Box 7 expenses on line 4 of Form 2106.

Then attach the Minister's Professional Expense Worksheet to your tax return. Just use the "Supporting Schedule for Form 2106" included in this manual. Make a copy of it, fill it out, enter your name and Social Security number and attach it to your tax return. Put all the expenses on line 4 of Form 2106.

(If you don't want to use the Minister's Professional Expense Worksheet as an attachment to your return, then enter all the expenses, except meals and entertainment, on line 4 of Form 2106. Then put meals and entertainment on line 5 of Form 2106.)

Do you have receipts for the expenses on this page?   ❏ yes   ❏ no

If you do have receipts, it is important to keep your receipts for expenses in a file marked "1998 expenses." If you do not have receipts for some items, they can still be deducted, but you should know that if your return is audited, they will probably be disallowed unless you kept an expense diary during the year. An "expense diary" can be as simple as a pocket calendar you use while traveling, in which you write the expense and amount on the day you paid it. Use it for expenses for less than $75 for which you don't have receipts.

Be sure you get reimbursements for all church-related expenses—a recent federal case says if you could have been reimbursed, but did not choose to, you may lose the right to deduct the expenses on your personal tax return.

Supporting Schedule to Form 2106

Minister's Professional Expense Worksheet
(*ClergyTax®* Box 7)

Name of Minister: _____

Social Security Number: _____ - _____ - _____

Educational expenses	$
Business telephone	$
Office supplies	$
Postage	$
Books	$
Tapes	$
Other religious materials	$
Tax return preparation	$
Seminars and dues	$
Subscriptions and fees	$
Office equipment	$
Post office box	$
Legal and accounting fees and expenses	$
Supplies (including vestments and cleaning)	$
Interest on charge cards used for business	$
Interest on auto loan(s) for cars used 100% for business	$
Business meals, entertainment and tips *X 50%*	$
Travel (auto rental; fares [air, train or bus]; hotel; laundry and cleaning; parking and tolls; telephone)	$
Interest on other business-related loan(s) (such as credit union, finance company, personal, educational, bank or life insurance loan)	$
Other:	$
Total:	$

Do you have receipts for your minister's professional expenses? If so, keep them in a separate folder, as these items are often checked by an IRS agent when auditing a minister's tax return.

Box 8

Box 8

1999 Itemized Deductions

Did you have any of the following deductions in 1999:

Please list the amount of any medical expenses you had in 1999, *which were not reimbursed by your church,* and not paid for by the insurance company. In other words, these are amounts you paid for *out of your own pocket* (to be deductible, items followed by an * must be related to a medical condition, or prescribed by a doctor).

1998 Medical Expenses

Insurance premiums	$
Medicare premiums	$
Prescriptions	$
Doctors	$
Dentists	$
Hospitals	$
Equipment (such as eyeglasses, dentures, hearing aids, special shoes, etc.)	$
Lab fees	$
Nursing costs	$
Medical supplies	$
Air conditioning*	$
Humidifier*	$
Electricity*	$
Transportation*	$
Hotel*	$
Other	$
Total Medical:	$

Box 8 Total Medical $ _____

This total goes on Schedule A, line 1.

Box 9

Box 9

A.   Real estate tax on your home:

$ _____

Enter this amount on Schedule A , line 6.

B.   Other property taxes paid:

$ _____

Enter this amount on Schedule A , line 7.

C.   Is there a number on either line 18 or line 21 of your W-2? This is state or local tax that was withheld from your salary on your church or other W-2.

$ _____

Did you pay state tax that was not on your W-2? (For example, check your 1998 state income tax return. If you owed state income tax when you filed your 1997 state return, and sent a check in with your 1998 state return, write the amount here):

$ _____

Total $ _____

Enter this amount on Schedule A , line 5.

Box 10

Box 10

Real estate mortgage loan interest on your home:

$ _____

Enter this amount on Schedule A , line 10.

Home equity loan interest:

$ _____

Enter this amount on Schedule A , line 10.

Instructions for Church Auto Worksheet

Each year, many pastors use a church-owned vehicle.

If personal mileage is allowed on a church-owned vehicle, some amount should be included on the pastor's W-2 at the end of year.

This amount is added both to line 12 of your W-2, and then also added to the amount of salary on line 1 of your W-2. In other words, *you add the same number to both lines.*

To find out how much to include on your W-2 for the personal use of a church auto, see the worksheet for church autos.

Annual Lease Value Worksheet

Fair Market Value of vehicle	$_____
Enter the Annual Lease Value (ALV) (See the Annual Lease Value Table)	$_____
Enter the amount of gasoline paid by the church during the year	$_____
Add the ALV and gasoline amount	$_____
Enter the amount of personal use	_____%
Multiple total ALV and gasoline by the % personal use	$_____

Enter the amount from the Annual Lease Value Worksheet on line 5 of the W-2 Income Worksheet.

Worksheet for Church Autos

Reproduced on the following page is the Annual Lease Value (or ALV) Table. Here's how you figure the correct amount to show on a minister's W-2 for personal use of a church auto:

Just look in column (1) to find the Auto Fair Market Value. This is what you paid for the car if it was purchased less than four years ago.

Then look across to column (2)—the corresponding amount is the auto's Annual Lease Value, or ALV.

Multiply the ALV times the percentage of personal use to find the amount that goes on the pastor's W-2.

If the church pays for gas, add 5.5 cents a mile to the W-2 for gas on personal miles. You can also use the actual cost of the gasoline, whichever you prefer.

Example: Let's say the auto cost $15,000. You can see that the ALV for $15,000 is $4,350. Let's say that the pastor used the car 10 percent for personal use. The correct amount to put on the W-2 is $435, or $4,350 times 10 percent. You also have to add gasoline. So let's say the church paid for $1,200 of gasoline during the year. Take $1,200 times 10 percent (the gasoline used for personal use), which amounts to $120. Add that to the use of the car, $435 + $120, and the cost is $555, the amount that goes on the W-2.

Let's say in line 1 of the W-2, $10,000 is listed as salary, and that line 12 is blank. Add $555 to both line 1 and line 12. So now line 1 will read $10,555, and line 12 will read $555.

You can prorate the ALV if the church owned the car less than the full year.

You should figure out the fair market value of the car again on January 1 after the fourth calendar year the car has been used. Use this value to find the new ALV (which will now be lower).

You can also use a new fair market value figure on January 1 of the year of transfer of a church auto from one staff person to another.

Let's say the church bought the car July 1, 1999, for $20,000. The ALV for each of the first four years (1999 prorated, 2000, 2001 and 2002) would be $5,600.

As of January 1, 2003, you would revalue the car at whatever it was worth on that date.

Let's say on January 1, 2003, the car is worth $10,000. Then the new ALV would be $3,100 for the next four years, and so on.

Annual Lease Value Table

Value of Car:	Annual Lease Value:
$ 0 - 999	$ 600
1,000 - 1,999	850
2,000 - 2,999	1,100
3,000 - 3,999	1,350
4,000 - 4,999	1,600
5,000 - 5,999	1,850
6,000 - 6,999	2,100
7,000 - 7,999	2,350
8,000 - 8,999	2,600
9,000 - 9,999	2,850
10,000 - 10,999	3,100
11,000 - 11,999	3,350
12,000 - 12,999	3,600
13,000 - 13,999	3,850
14,000 - 14,999	4,100
15,000 - 15,999	4,350
16,000 - 16,999	4,600
17,000 - 17,999	4,850
18,000 - 18,999	5,100
19,000 - 19,999	5,350
20,000 - 20,999	5,600
21,000 - 21,999	5,850
22,000 - 22,999	6,100
23,000 - 23,999	6,350
24,000 - 24,999	6,600
25,000 - 25,999	6,850
26,000 - 27,999	7,250
28,000 - 29,999	7,750
30,000 - 31,999	8,250
32,000 - 33,999	8,750
34,000 - 35,999	9,250
36,000 - 37,999	9,750
38,000 - 39,999	10,250
40,000 - 41,999	10,750
42,000 - 43,999	11,250
44,000 - 45,999	11,750
46,000 - 47,999	12,250
48,000 - 49,999	12,750
50,000 - 51,999	13,250
52,000 - 53,999	13,750
54,000 - 55,999	14,250
56,000 - 57,999	14,750
58,000 - 59,999	15,250
60,000 - up	.25 X auto fair market value + $500

Example:

Annual Lease Value Worksheet

Fair Market Value of vehicle	$12,500
Enter the Annual Lease Value (ALV) (See the Annual Lease Value Table at left)	$ 3,600
Enter the amount of gasoline paid by the church during the year	$ 1,500
Add the ALV and gasoline amount	$ 5,100
Enter the amount of personal use	15%
Multiply total ALV and gasoline by the % personal use ($5,100 X 0.15)	$ 765

➥ Put this amount on line 5 of the W-2 Income Worksheet in the instructions for Box 1.
        - or -
➥ Put this amount in Box 12 of the W-2, and also *add* the same amount to Box 1 of the W-2.

Auto Expense Worksheet

Put the number on Form 2106 on the lines indicated.

Auto Information	Car #1	Car #2
Year and make		
Date of purchase	Line 11a	Line 11b
Purchase price	Line 30a	Line 30b
Total miles for 1998	Line 12a	Line 12b
Business miles for 1998	Line 13a	Line 13b
Expenses:		
Gasoline	$	$
Insurance, auto club	$	$
License and registration	$	$
Auto excise and sales taxes	$	$
Parking and tolls	$	$
Oil, service and repairs	$	$
Tires and batteries	$	$
Washing and waxing	$	$
Totals:	$ Line 23a	$ Line 23b

Note: If you're filing a Schedule C, these totals go on line 10 of Schedule C. Also remember to figure depreciation for your car(s) used for business on line 13 of Schedule C.

Box 11

Box 11

Business Auto Mileage

Number of miles you drove on church business in 1999: _____ miles

➡ Enter this number on Part II, line 22 of Form 2106. The mileage rate for 1999 is 31 cents a mile. (Yes, alert reader, the mileage allowance actually *went down* for 1999. The IRS adopted a new way of figuring the allowance which caused it to be less for 1999 than it was for 1998.) The new rate starts on April 1, 1999.

➡ To use actual auto expenses as a deduction, use the Auto Expense Worksheet. Multiply total auto expenses by percentage of business use to find the amount you can deduct.

Box 12

Box 12

Charitable Contributions Deduction

A.   Cash Contributions to your church

$ _____

Enter this amount on Schedule A , line 15.

B.   Is the total amount of cash contributions to your church in Box A more than $1,000?

❑ yes   ❑ no

If yes, you should probably attach to your return a copy of the letter your church sent you that verifies the total amount of your contributions for 1999. In addition, if you made one or more separate contributions of $250+ to your church, you should be sure the church gives you a letter listing your total contributions. (The IRS has responded to comments from churches that found it a hardship to keep records for every donation of $250 or more that came in. IRS regulations have now been modified to state that where a donor makes several $250 contributions in a given year to a church, one giving statement showing the *total amount* of the donor's contributions for the year will satisfy IRS rules.)

C.   Cash contributions to other ministries

$ _____

Enter this amount on Schedule A, line 15.

D.   Cash contributions to be carried over from last year

$ _____

Enter this amount on Schedule A, line 17.

E.   Cash contributions to be carried over to next year

$ _____

Make a record of this number, then enter this amount on Schedule A, line 17 of your *2000 tax return* (next year's return).

F.   Value of non-cash contributions, such as clothes, supplies, furniture, jewelry, etc.

$ _____

Enter this amount on Schedule A, line 16.

If the value is more than $500, you'll need to fill out and attach Form 8283 to your return (see IRS instructions).

Part 2
Items That May Not Apply to All Pastors

Many ministers don't have to deal with these areas, but if you do, you will find the instructions you need as indicated in the section following this one. Scan down this index. You only need to complete the items that relate to you.

Here's the best way to handle this section:

First, "ski" down the list. As you go, mark the box in the middle column next to any item you think you might need.

Now, you only have to deal with items that have an *X* by them.

Take them one at a time, and check the details on that item (just match the number of the item in the series of pages that follows this checklist), in this handy format:

Do you have an item/situation like this? Check this box. Then go to...

Then ➥ You're done! Congratulations!

We've also included a final checklist before you file your return (following this section) to help you be sure you didn't miss anything.

If you have an item on this list, the page number tells you where to look for further instructions for completing the numbered item.

If the minister... (*during the 1999 tax year*)	Check Box	Then go to...
1. Didn't get a Form W-2 at all	❑	page 34
2. Had personal use of the church auto	❑	page 34
3. Needs an extension to file the 1999 tax return	❑	page 34
4. Received a Partnership, Estate or Corporation Form K-1	❑	page 35
5. Received pension benefits or annuities	❑	page 35
6. Received royalties	❑	page 35
7. Rendered baby-sitting services and/or had other odd jobs	❑	page 35
8. Received a state income tax refund during 1999	❑	page 35
9. Paid someone to care for his/her children so the minister could work (includes payments to the church daycare center)	❑	page 35
10. Received Social Security payments	❑	page 35
11. Received child support payments	❑	page 36
12. Received alimony payments	❑	page 36
13. Had his wife and/or children travel with him on church business at church expense	❑	page 36
14. Purchased personal items such as clothes, jewelry, furniture, electronics and other similar items directly from church funds	❑	page 36
15. Received personal funds directly from petty cash or from church offerings	❑	page 36
16. Had his or her own business in 1999 (that is, did anything on the side where you earned extra money)	❑	page 36
17. Had investments in the stock market	❑	page 36

18. Sold a major item for cash or on an installment sale   ❑   page 37

If the minister... (*during the 1999 tax year*)	Check Box	Then go to...
19. Owned rental property and received rent from tenants	❑	page 37
20. Received income from bartering goods and/or services	❑	page 37
21. Made a one-time gift greater than $10,000 to an individual	❑	page 37
22. Had a casualty or theft loss that was not covered by insurance	❑	page 37
23. Marital status changed	❑	page 37
24. Incurred ministry-related educational expenses	❑	page 37
25. Received notices and/or settled an IRS audit	❑	page 37
26. Had any of the following deductions:	❑	page 38

    A.   Donations to the district office of the minister's denomination

    B.   Contributions to colleges or universities

    C.   Personal property tax

    D.   Alimony paid

    E.   Job-hunting expenses

27. Gave any of the following items to charity: ❑   page 38

    A.   Auto mileage

    B.   Other travel expenses

    C.   Clothing

    D.   Furniture

    E.   Supplies for charity

    F.   Jewelry

    G.   Real estate

    H.   Coins

    I.   Any other non-cash item

    J.   Was the total of your non-cash donations in 1999 more than $500?

28. Made contributions (including spouse's) to an IRA (Individual Retirement Account) or other pension plan	❑	page 38
29. Made withdrawals from an IRA or other pension plan	❑	page 39
30. Made rollovers from one IRA or other pension plan to another	❑	page 39
31. The church made contributions to an IRA or other pension plan (such as a 403(b) Plan) for you in 1999	❑	page 39
32. Received paid health-related expenses from the church (including insurance premiums) yet the minister was issued a Form 1099 instead of a Form W-2	❑	page 39
33. Refinanced his/her home since January 1, 1999	❑	page 40
34. Moved from one residence to another	❑	page 40
35. Purchased or sold a home	❑	page 40
36. Sold other real estate	❑	page 40
37. Had an office in his/her home that was used exclusively for church business	❑	page 40
38. Had a capital loss carryover from last year	❑	page 41

39. Received a Form 1099 from the church ❏ page 41

If the minister... (*during the 1999 tax year*)	**Check Box**	**Then go to...**
40. *Did* have Social Security tax withheld from his/her paycheck	❏	page 41
41. Had *no* income tax withheld from his/her paycheck	❏	page 42
42. Paid estimated tax each quarter	❏	page 42
43. Wants (or spouse) $3 to go to the Presidential Election Campaign Fund	❏	page 42
44. Filed *no* income tax return last year	❏	page 42
45. Is *not* ordained or licensed, or not yet Social Security exempt	❏	page 42
46. Is exempt from Social Security tax (or spouse is exempt) because the minister or spouse has filed a valid Form 4361)	❏	page 43
47. Is taking a tax return position that is aggressive, or where the facts are not conclusive	❏	page 43
48. Lives in a state that has a state income tax return	❏	page 43
49. Do you have any other kind of income?	❏	page 44
50. Do you need to see a list of nontaxable kinds of income?	❏	page 44

Explanation of Checklist 1-50

Item 1: No Form W-2 Received

But what if you didn't get a W-2 at all? There's still hope: you can use Form 4852 instead. Get Form 4852 from the IRS, and fill in the blanks using the information from Box 1 (or from the Box 1 W-2 Income Worksheet) for the amount that should have been on your W-2. .

Item 2: Personal Use of Church Auto

If the church provided a car for you during 1999, if the church owns your car, and you have personal use of the church auto, then you'll need to use the Annual Lease Value Table in the Church Auto Worksheet, but you won't need to make any other entries on your tax return about your car. (You don't need to use the Church Auto Worksheet if the church has already included the amount for personal use of the church auto on your W-2 or 1099).

Please answer the two questions below:

1. Did the church provide a car for you in 1999?   ❑ yes ❑ no

    a.   If yes, does your church have a written policy about
        church-owned cars in the church minutes?   ❑ yes ❑ no
        If yes, Great!

  If no, you need to write up minutes for this.

    b.   If yes, did the church include any amount for personal
        use on your W-2 or 1099 because of the car?   ❑ yes ❑ no
        If yes, you don't need to use the Church Auto Worksheet.
        If no, you need to include the personal use of the car on your tax return.

2. Did the church give you any other type of auto allowance in 1999?

> Amount $_____

If you turned in a record of your miles, and the church reimbursed you at 31 cents a mile, you don't have to report this as income. But if the church just paid you a *cash auto allowance* and didn't ask you for any receipts, then you have to report the cash allowance as income. If your cash auto allowance is not already on your W-2 or 1099, then enter this amount on line 21 of Form 1040, page 1. Under "Description," put "cash auto allowance." If you are not Social Security tax exempt, also enter this amount on Schedule SE, line 2. (Don't carry this amount to Schedule SE if you have filed Form 4361 to be exempt from Social Security tax.)

If the church did not provide a car, please use the Auto Expense Worksheet to fill in your car expenses. Enter these expenses on Form 2106, line 23. (If you get a 1099, enter these expenses on Schedule C.)

Do you have written receipts for these expenses?   ❑ yes ❑ no
Do you have a mileage log to prove business mileage?   ❑ yes ❑ no

If you don't have an auto log, or written receipts, and if your return is audited, you can expect an IRS examiner to want proof of these expenses. That doesn't mean you can't deduct them, it just means that you could be asked to back up your auto expense deductions.

Item 3: Filing Extensions

If you can't file your tax return on or before April 17, 2000, then you need to file an extension on Form 4868 until August 15, 2000. You will still have to pay your tax on April 17, 2000, even if you file an extension, but you will have more time to get your information together.

If you can't file your tax return on or before August 15, 2000, you can file a second extension on Form 2688 until October 16, 2000. (The second extension is not granted automatically, although the first one usually is.)

➥ **Always use certified mail, <u>return receipt requested</u>, to file any extension(s).**

Item 4: Partnership, Estate or Corporation Form K-1

If you received a Partnership, Estate or Corporation Form K-1:

    Enter these amounts on Form 1040 and accompanying Schedules, according to the instructions you received with your K-1.

Item 5: Pension Benefits or Annuities

For Pensions or Annuities, you'll need the Form 1099R or Form W-2P you received:

Name of Bank or Company	Amount
_____	$ _____
_____	$ _____
_____	$ _____

    Enter these amounts on Form 1040, line 16a. (Carry any taxable amount to line 16b.)

Item 6: Royalties

Royalties $ _____

    Enter these on Schedule E, line 4.

Item 7: Baby-sitting and/or Other Odd Jobs Income

Baby-sitting, odd jobs $ _____

    Enter these on line 21 of Form 1040, page 1.

    (Carry to Schedule SE, line 2 if you are *not* Social Security exempt and the income was *not* ministry related.)

Item 8: State Income Tax Refund

State income tax refund $ _____ *

    Enter this amount on line 10 of Form 1040, page 1.

    *You should check your income tax return for last year to see if you have to include this amount as income this year; a state income tax refund is income only under certain circumstances. If you couldn't deduct your state tax on last year's Schedule A, you may not have to include your state refund as income in 1999.

Item 9: Payments for Child-Care Services

Did you pay anyone to care for your children so you could work in 1998?   ❏ yes   ❏ no

    If yes, use Form 2441 for the child-care credit.

    There is a new adoption credit (see appendix 3).

Item 10: Social Security Payments

Social Security payments $ _____

    Enter these on line 20a of Form 1040, page 1. (Carry any taxable amount to line 20b.)

    (Sometimes these are nontaxable, and sometimes partially or fully taxable. Tax preparation software will figure this for you automatically.)

Item 11: Child-Support Payments
Child-support or child-care payments $ _____
>These are nontaxable and do not have to be reported on your return.

Item 12: Alimony Payments Received
Alimony payments received $ _____
>Enter these on Form 1040, line 11.

Item 13: Family Members Travel at Church Expense
As pastor, have your wife or children ever traveled with you on church business at church expense?

>If yes, the extra amounts spent for your wife and children are taxable, and should be reported on your W-2. If you have this type of income, and it's not on your W-2, put it on line 21 of Form 1040, page 1. (Carry to Schedule SE, line 2 if you are *not* Social Security exempt.) You only have to include the extra amount—for example, if your wife stays in the same hotel room you would have had anyway, there is no extra income; but if she needs a separate plane ticket, this amount is reportable as income. Unless, your wife works with you in the ministry and was with you on church business. If so, then these items don't have to be reported.

Item 14: Purchase of Personal Items with Church Funds
Have you ever purchased personal items such as clothes, jewelry, furniture, electronics, etc. directly from church funds?

>If yes, these amounts are taxable, and should be reported as income on your W-2. If you have this type of income, and it's not on your W-2, put it on line 21 of Form 1040, page 1. (Carry to Schedule SE, line 2 if you are *not* Social Security exempt.)

Item 15: Receipt of Personal Funds from Church Petty Cash or Church Offerings
Have you ever received personal funds directly from petty cash, or from church offerings?

>If yes, these amounts are taxable, and should be reported as income on your W-2. If you have this type of income, and it's not on your W-2, put it on line 21 of Form 1040, page 1. (Carry to Schedule SE, line 2 if you are *not* Social Security exempt.)

Item 16: Separate Business Activity
Did you have your own business in 1999 (that is, did you do anything on the side where you earned money)?

    ❏ yes   ❏ no

>If yes, please use Schedule C and attach it to your tax return.
>If yes, do you have an office in your home that you used exclusively for this business in 1999?   ❏ yes   ❏ no
>If yes, use Form 8829 and attach it to your Schedule C at line 30.

Item 17: Investments in the Stock Market
Did you have any investments in the stock market in 1999?   ❏ yes   ❏ no
>If yes, please use the Schedule D form for gains or losses.

Item 18: Sale of a Major Item for Cash or an Installment Sale

Did you sell any kind of major item for cash or on an installment sale in 1999? (That is, where the person you sold it to is making payments to you each month; this could be a house, car, boat or other major item.)

❑ yes   ❑ no

If yes, you may have to use Form 6252.

Item 19: Rental Property Ownership and Rental Income

Did you own any rental property in 1999 and receive rent from tenants?

❑ yes   ❑ no

If yes, please use "Schedule E" and attach it to your tax return.

Item 20: Bartering for Goods and/or Services

Did you receive any income from bartering goods or services in 1999? ❑ yes   ❑ no

If yes, please list it on Form 1040, page 1, line 21. (In some cases, you may need to carry this amount to Schedule SE, line 2 if you are *not* Social Security exempt.)

Item 21: One-Time Gift Greater Than $10,000 to an Individual

Did you make any gift over $10,000 in 1999 to an individual?   ❑ yes   ❑ no

If yes, you probably need to file a gift-tax return. This is Form 709, and the IRS will send you a copy if you call 1-800-TAX FORM.

Item 22: Casualty and/or Theft Losses

Did you have any casualty or theft losses in 1999 that were not covered by insurance?

❑ yes   ❑ no

If yes, please use Form 4684.

Item 23: Change in Marital Status

Did your marital status change in 1999?   ❑ yes   ❑ no

If yes, please indicate date married _____, or date divorced _____, or date spouse died _____ and see the IRS Form 1040 instructions.

Item 24: Ministry-Related Educational Expenses

Did you incur educational expenses in 1999 to help you do your job better?

❑ yes   ❑ no

If yes, did the church pay for these? (If so, they may be tax-free up to $5,250 for 1998. At present, Congress has extended this benefit through May 31, 2000. However, it does not currently apply to graduate courses. Legislation is currently pending that would apply the exclusion for church-provided education assistance, for both graduate and undergraduate education, to courses beginning on or before June 30, 2004.)

If no, you may deduct them on Form 2106, line 4.

Item 25: IRS Notices or Settlements

During 1999, did you receive notices or settle any IRS audits?   ❑ yes   ❑ no

If yes, are you using any changes agreed to for your audited return on this year's return? If not, these items are likely to be challenged again. On the other hand, if you were previously audited for the past two years with no changes to your return, you shouldn't be audited again for a while. (But if you are, discuss the matter with a tax attorney or Certified Public Accountant.)

Item 26: Donations, Property Tax, Alimony and/or Job-Hunting Expenses

Did you have any of these deductions in 1999?

    A. Donations to the district office (or whatever they call it) of your denomination

        ❏ yes   ❏ no

Note: A recent case says that if you are expected to make "donations" or "tithe" to your denomination to remain in good standing as a minister, then you can deduct these expenses both on Schedule A and on Schedule SE if you get a W-2 (or, if you get a 1099, on Schedule C). However, you can expect the IRS to ask questions about whether you really are obligated to make these "contributions." True charitable donations to your church, which are given for the sole reason that you want to give them, can only be deducted on Schedule A.

    B. Contributions made to colleges and/or universities ❏ yes   ❏ no
       Enter on Schedule A, line 15
    C. Personal property tax ❏ yes   ❏ no
       Enter on Schedule A, line 7
    D. Alimony paid ❏ yes   ❏ no
       Enter on Form 1040, Page 1, line 31a
    E. Job-hunting expenses ❏ yes   ❏ no
       Enter on Schedule A, line 20

Item 27: Non-Cash Charitable Contributions

Did you give any of these items to charity in 1999? ❏ yes   ❏ no
Enter the total from the following worksheet for each of the items on Schedule A, on line 16:

    A. Auto mileage _____ miles X 14 cents [line 16]
    B. Other travel expenses $ _____ [line 16]
    C. Clothing $ _____ [line 16]
    D. Furniture $ _____ [line 16]
    E. Supplies for charity $ _____ [line 16]
    F. Jewelry $ _____ [line 16]
    G. Real estate $ _____ [line 16]
    H. Coins $ _____ [line 16]
    I. Other _____ $ _____
          Total $ _____ [include on line 16]

    J. If the total of your non-cash donations in 1999 was more than $500, please fill out Form 8283 (see IRS instructions for this form).

Item 28: Minister's (or Spouse) Contributions to an IRA or Other Pension Plan.

Did you (or your spouse) make any contributions to an IRA in 1999?

        ❏ yes   ❏ no

If you made an IRA contribution, this should be entered on line 23 of Form 1040, page 1.

If your spouse made an IRA contribution, enter it on line 23 of Form 1040, page 1.

Did you (or your spouse) make any contributions to some other kind of pension plan in 1999?

❏ yes   ❏ no

If the minister, (or the church), made contributions to a church pension plan [403b Plan], these amounts do not have to be reported on the minister's tax return, unless the minister or the church made more than the maximum contribution allowable. Contributions to a Section 403(b) church retirement plan may be shown on line 13 of the minister's Form W-2, even though this amount is not taxable.

Item 29: Withdrawals from an IRA or Other Pension Plan

Did you or your spouse make any withdrawals from an IRA or other pension plan (such as a church 403(b) plan) in 1999?   ❏ yes   ❏ no

If yes, enter IRA withdrawals on Form 1040, page 1, line 15a. Carry any taxable portion to line 15b.

If yes, enter pension withdrawals on Form 1040, page 1, line 16a. Carry any taxable portion to line 16b.

Item 30: IRA or Other Pension Plan Rollovers

Did you make any rollovers from one IRA or other pension plan to another in 1999?   ❏ yes   ❏ no

If yes, enter these on Form 1040, page 1, line 15a. Unless these were taxable for some reason, line 15b will be "0."

Item 31: Church-Paid IRA or Other Pension Plan Contributions

Did the church make any contributions to an IRA or other pension plan (such as a 403(b) Plan) for you in 1999?

❏ yes   ❏ no

If you, or the church, made contributions to a church pension plan [403b Plan], you don't have to report these on your tax return, unless you or the church made more than the maximum contribution allowable. Although some CPAs believe it's not an IRS requirement to do so, 403(b) church retirement plan contributions can be shown on line 13 of your W-2, even though they aren't taxable. Use the letter *E* and the amount. For example, if the church made a $5,000 contribution for you to the church 403(b) retirement plan, then on line 13 on your W-2 write "E-5000."

Note: On the other hand, contributions directly from the church to an IRA you own are taxable, and should be shown on your W-2. (If these contributions are not reported on the minister's Form W-2, they should be listed on line 21 of Form 1040.) You can then deduct these payments on your tax return, subject to the standard IRA limits.

Item 32: Church-Paid Health Insurance Premiums and Receipt of a Form 1099

Did the church pay any health insurance premiums for you in 1999?

❏ yes   ❏ no

If yes, these are tax-free as long as you get a W-2 and not a 1099 from your church.

If yes, has your church adopted a church health expense policy in the minutes?

❏ yes   ❏ no

If the church is going to pay your health insurance premiums, or reimburse you as a minister for your out-of-pocket health-related expenses, it is important that you have a written health expense policy in the church minutes. Sample minutes are included in this book.

If no, that is, if the church paid your health insurance premiums and issued to you a Form 1099 for your church salary, then report the amount of insurance premiums paid by the church on line 1 of Schedule C.

Item 33: Refinancing of the Minister's Home

Have you refinanced your home since January 1, 1999?   ❏ yes   ❏ no

If yes, please see IRS Form 1040 instructions for how to handle points and other possible deductions. This work area will help you assemble the information you will need:

Amount of loan	$ _____
Cost of regular housing items	$ _____
Cost of any improvements	$ _____
Proceeds used for education	$ _____
Proceeds used for medical expenses	$ _____
Amount of points	$ _____

Did you pay the points by separate check?   ❏ yes   ❏ no

Item 34: Moving Expenses

Did you move in 1999?   ❏ yes   ❏ no
If yes, please use the Moving Expenses Form 3903.

Item 35: Sale or Purchase of a Home

Did you buy or sell your home in 1999?   ❏ Bought   ❏ Sold

If yes, please use Form 2119 (see IRS instructions).

Note: Please review a copy of your closing statement(s) because it will often show listings of deductible taxes, interest and possibly other items.

If you sold your home for more than you paid for it, you have two years to buy another home that costs at least as much as the home you sold, or you will have to pay capital gains tax on the home you sold.

Item 36: Sale of Other Real Estate

Did you sell real estate (other than your personal residence) in 1999?   ❏ yes   ❏ no

If yes, please use Schedule D (see IRS instructions).

Item 37: Home Office Used Exclusively for Church Business

Do you have an office in your home that you used exclusively for church business in 1999?

❏ yes   ❏ no

If yes, do you use this home office for church-related work you cannot do at your regular church office (either because you don't have a regular church office, or for some other reason)?   ❏ yes   ❏ no

If yes, do you commute daily between this office and the main church office?

❏ yes   ❏ no

If yes, what is the approximate mileage between your home office and the church office? _____

If yes, what is the approximate square footage in your house? _____ sq. ft.; and what is the approximate square footage of your home office? _____ sq. ft.

Note: If you spent more money on housing expenses than the church gave you for housing, you may be able to deduct some of the money you spent because you have a home office. Just know that the IRS looks at this area closely.

If you can deduct these expenses, then enter these expenses on Schedule C, line 30, and fill out your home office expenses on Form 8829 and attach it to your return.

Note: Even if you can't deduct expenses for a home office, for example, because you also have an office at the church and there is no compelling reason for you to have an office at home other than personal convenience, you possibly may be able to deduct your auto mileage from your home office to your church office (although the rules here are unclear). Just because you may be able to deduct your auto mileage between your two offices still does not mean you can deduct your home office expenses.

Note: If you have a computer in your home office, be sure you can show that you use it for church business, and that the church allows you to keep it at home because they get more work out of you that way. If you can't show this, expect the IRS to ask you for a log of your computer use, which they will use to try to disallow any personal use of the computer. One way around this problem is to make an entry in the church minute book that says the church owns the computer, not you, and that the computer may not be used for personal use.

New home office rules: Due to a new tax law, a minister now qualifies for a home office deduction if: (1) the office is used by the minister to conduct administrative or management activities of a church or ministry, and (2) there is no other fixed location where the minister conducts substantial administrative or management activities of the church or ministry. As under present law, deductions will be allowed for a home office meeting the above two-part test only if the office is exclusively used on a regular basis for church or ministry business by the minister and, in the case of a minister who is an employee, only if such exclusive use is for the convenience of the church. This new rule applies beginning January 1, 1999.

Item 38: Capital Loss Carryover

Do you have a capital loss carryover from last year?   ❑ yes   ❑ no

If yes, enter this on Schedule D. Use either line 6 or line 15, whichever applies.

Item 39: Receipt of a Church-Issued Form 1099

Did you receive a church 1099 for 1999?   ❑ yes   ❑ no

If yes, be sure to read appendix 2, 1099s carefully. Usually, you do not need to attach a 1099 to your tax return, unless it shows that income tax was withheld from the money you received.

Enter the number from line 7 of your 1099(s) on Schedule C, line 1.

Note: Sometimes a church will give a minister a W-2 for regular salary, and also issue a 1099 for other income, such as a "love offering," honorariums, etc. In cases like this where the only entry on a Schedule C would be the income, and there are no expenses to be deducted against that income (perhaps because the church has an accountable reimbursement plan), then there is no reason not to show the W-2 income on line 7 of the 1040, and the 1099 income on line 21 of the 1040.

In fact, even if you do have expenses to deduct, you can still use line 21 for your 1099 income. Then you deduct your expenses from your Schedule SE income, and take the 2 percent "hit" on Schedule A. You will lower your audit risk by as much as five times, at a total cost of the 2 percent difference on Schedule A. Even if the IRS challenges this approach (which is about as likely as a crow flying backward), it will only work in your favor because you will then pick up the 2 percent difference. Some accountants won't like what I just said, but remember, the only person more boring than an accountant is an economist. What do you get when you cross an economist with the godfather? An offer you can't understand.

In addition, the Form 1099 amount should be reported on Schedule SE (long form) *only if* the minister is *not* Social Security exempt.

Item 40: Social Security Tax Withheld from Minister's Paycheck

Did the church withhold Social Security tax from your paycheck on lines 4 or 6?

❑ yes   ❑ no

If yes, your W-2, if any, will be incorrect, and should be corrected (file form W-2c to correct W-2s for ministers in appendix 1).

Item 41: No Income Tax Withholding on Minister's Paycheck

Did the church withhold income tax from your paycheck?   ❑ yes   ❑ no

If no, it is okay because ministers are exempt from income tax withholding. However, it is usually best to be on voluntary withholding, so you don't owe tax at the end of the year. If you don't have voluntary withholding, then you should be paying an estimated tax each quarter.

If yes, did you pay estimated tax each quarter?   ❑ yes   ❑ no

Item 42: Estimated Quarterly Tax Payments

If you paid estimated tax, write down how much you paid each quarter:

Date	Federal Tax Paid	Date	State Tax Paid	Date
1st Quarter, due date 4/15/99	$ _____	_____	$ _____	_____
2nd Quarter, due date 6/16/99	$ _____	_____	$ _____	_____
3rd Quarter, due date 9/15/99	$ _____	_____	$ _____	_____
4th Quarter, due date 1/17/00	$ _____	_____	$ _____	_____

Please note: Do not include amounts paid with your 1998 tax return (filed 4/15/99), or amounts paid in response to an IRS notice. The above are amounts paid toward your 1999 income tax. Please check this carefully.

Enter your estimated tax payments on line 58 of Form 1040, page 2.

Enter total estimated state tax payments on line 5 of Schedule A for Form 1040.

Please note: If you did not pay enough tax during the year, you will owe an underpayment penalty.

Don't overlook payments you may have made if you filed an extension(s) for your return:

❑ Form 4868—Extension $_____ (Enter here the amount of any tax you sent in with your first extension.) Enter extension payments on Form 1040, page 2, line 61.

❑ Form 2688—Extension $_____ (Enter here the amount of any tax you sent in with your second extension.) Enter extension payments on Form 1040, page 2, line 61.

Item 43: Presidential Election Campaign Fund

Do you want $3 to go to the Presidential Election Campaign Fund?   ❑ yes   ❑ no

Check the box near the top of Form 1040, page 1, under your name, to the right.

If you are married, does your husband or wife want $3 to go to this fund?   ❑ yes   ❑ no

Check the box near the top of Form 1040, page 1, under your name, to the right.

Item 44: No Income Tax Return Filed

Did you file an income tax return last year?   ❑ yes   ❑ no

If no, and you had income above the threshold for filing a return, you probably need to consult a competent tax professional IMMEDIATELY.

Item 45: Nonordained, Unlicensed or Not Yet Social Security Exempt Ministers

Are you ordained or licensed as a minister?   ❑ yes   ❑ no

If no, you cannot exclude housing allowance, and you must have income tax and Social Security tax (FICA) withheld from your paycheck.

If yes, please give date: _____

Name of ordaining church or ministry: _____

What was the first year you were paid for services as a minister? _____ If the answer is 1998, 1999 or 2000, you can still qualify to file an exemption from Social Security tax. **Note**: If the answer is 1998, you only have until April 17, 2000, to file the exemption.

➡ However, filing a valid extension on Form 4868 will extend your time to file the exemption to August 15, 2000, and then filing Form 2688 may extend the date to October 16, 2000, but this isn't guaranteed because this second extension isn't automatically granted. ➡ **Always use <u>certified mail, return receipt requested,</u> to file any extension(s).**

If the answer is any other previous year, and the *second year* you were paid for services as a minister is 1999 or 2000, you may still qualify to file the exemption, assuming you meet all the other requirements. You may also be able to file this exemption if you changed churches in 1998, 1999 or 2000, were reordained, and have had a change of religious belief about receiving Social Security benefits on your earnings as a minister. See end of appendix 5.

Item 46: Exemption from Social Security Tax—Minister (or Minister's Spouse)

Are you exempt from Social Security tax, that is, have you ever filed Form 4361 (Minister's Exemption from Social Security tax)?   ❏ yes   ❏ no

If yes, please be sure you have a copy of your approval(s) from IRS in a safe place, and keep extra copies in other locations where you can find them if an auditor should ever want to see your approved copy. Then, be sure to write "Exempt - Form 4361" on the dotted part of line 50 of Form 1040, page 2.

Has your spouse ever filed Form 4361?   ❏ yes   ❏ no

If yes, please be sure you have a copy of your approval(s) from IRS in a safe place, and keep extra copies in other locations where you can find them if an auditor should ever want to see your approved copy. Then, be sure to write "Exempt - Form 4361" on the dotted part of line 50 of Form 1040, page 2.

Any non-ministry related (i.e., secular) income continues to be subject to Social Security taxes (see end of appendix 3, and end of appendix 5).

Item 47: Aggressive Tax Return Position

Are you taking a tax return position that is aggressive, or where the facts are not conclusive?

If so, fully disclose the facts and your position using a separate piece of paper attached to your tax return. This can lower audit risk, and may head off penalties if you are later questioned by the IRS about this item.

Item 48: State Income Tax

Does your state have an income tax return? If so, you can usually use the information you've already filled out, and carry it over to your state return.

State Tax Information

This is some of the information you will probably need when filling out your state tax return:

Please give the name of your school district _____

Please give the county you work in, if it is different from the county you live in _____

For states that have a rent credit (look in the instructions for your state tax return to see if your state has a rent credit):

If you paid rent on your home in 1999, please give the number of months in 1999 that you paid rent: _____ Monthly rent: $ _____

Please give your landlord's name and address:

Name _____

Address _____

City, State, Zip _____

(If you want to do your state return by hand, and didn't receive a package of blank state forms, please go to your state revenue office and get a complete package of blank 1999 income tax forms for your state. The package contains information you may need when filling out your state income tax return.)

When filling out your state return, be alert for state credits such as:

> property tax credit
> credit for federal Social Security tax paid
> credit for federal income tax paid
> educational expense or job training credit
> school tuition credit
> various environmental and wildlife credits
> donation of computers to schools credit
> other types of contributions credits

Many states have credits that are not the same as, or are more generous than, federal income tax credits. Tax preparation software can help you identify these credits more easily.

Item 49: Other Income
Did you have any other income not described above?   ❑ yes   ❑ no
    Other _____ $ _____
    If yes, please look in the IRS instructions to find out how to handle it.

Item 50: Items of "Income" on Which You Don't Have to Pay Tax
Are you wondering if an item should have gone in the W-2 Income Worksheet in Box 1? Here are some items you don't have to pay tax on if you get a W-2:

Here is what is not included in Box 1:

1. *Housing allowance*, as long as you spent all of it on housing items.
2. *Auto mileage reimbursements*, as long as you turned in your business miles to the church treasurer, and got paid 31 cents a mile. (The mileage allowance for 1999 actually went down, because the IRS adopted a new way of figuring the allowance. The old rate for 1998 was 32.5 cents a mile; the new rate for 1999 is only 31 cents.)
3. *Business use of the church auto you drove on church business* (although keeping an auto log is not a legal requirement, the IRS will probably challenge your mileage if you don't have a written log to prove it).
4. *Health insurance premiums* (as long as you get a W-2 instead of a 1099).
5. *Health expense reimbursements*, including payment of insurance deductibles, co-insurance amounts, and any other out-of-pocket expenses (as long as you get a W-2 instead of a 1099).
    Note: It is possible that reimbursements of out-of-pocket health costs may be income, depending on how the IRS eventually interprets this benefit. Normally, churches can pay health insurance premiums for the pastor, even if other staff are not covered, and the benefit is still tax-free (although it wouldn't be if this were done by a for-profit corporation). The law is less clear when it comes to reimbursements of out-of-pocket health costs. If these are paid for all staff, there shouldn't be a problem; but if they are paid for the pastor only, and not for other staff, it is possible IRS could say these reimbursements are income. By next year, hopefully, Congress will have clarified this point.
6. *Retirement plan contributions made by the church.* These can be tax free up to $30,000. Figure that the church can contribute an amount equal to about 25 percent of your total compensation to a 403(b) Church Retirement Plan. These plans are highly technical, and a competent

tax professional should be consulted for advice. (See the book *Retirement Plans for Ministers* for an overview of these plans. Many retirement rules for ministers have recently changed.)

7. *Retirement plan contributions made by salary reduction agreements.* These can be tax free up to $10,000. Figure that you can contribute an amount equal to about 20 percent of your total compensation to a 403(b) Church Retirement Plan. These plans are highly technical, and a competent tax professional should be consulted for advice. (Note: Salary reduction plans may be subject to FICA withholding for *non-minister* employees only. See the book *Retirement Plans for Ministers* for an overview of these plans. Many retirement rules for ministers have recently changed.)

But note: The church pays a 7.65 percent share of FICA and Medicare taxes for *non-minister* employees only (this is the amount the church "matches" for a non-minister; it is not part of the employee's wages). **Churches are not supposed to match FICA for ministers.** It is income to the minister if this happens. If the church has matched FICA and Medicare tax on your W-2 as a minister, you need to amend your W-2 (this can sometimes result in a refund).

Other Fringe Benefits That Are *Not* Taxable:

Group term life insurance (up to $50,000 face amount)

Disability insurance

Reimbursements of church expenses (under an accountable plan)

Cafeteria plans in some cases

Church-paid child care (or disabled dependent-care services) up to $5,000

Education assistance (up to $5,250) (currently extended to May 31, 2000; may be extended to June 30, 2004)

Church-provided legal services (where necessary to comply with IRS rules for churches)

On-premises athletic facilities

De *minimus* fringe benefits:

$65 a month of bus, train or limousine "transit pass" fares

Occasional supper money and/or taxi fare when you work overtime

Low-value holiday gifts, such as a turkey or ham

Long distance telephone calls

Picnics and Christmas parties

Occasional tickets to sports events

Free coffee and snacks

Use of the copy machine

Free postage stamps

Use of secretarial services for personal items

Church cafeteria

Employee discounts

Qualified tuition reductions (check to see if extended)

Working Condition Fringe Benefits:

Subscriptions to religious publications

Business use of your car

Educational expenses related to being a minister or other church staff job (this can include seminars and other church meetings)

Parking fees, if you have to pay to park near work, up to $175 a month

Membership and dues in professional associations

Seminars, conventions, classes

All types of materials and supplies related to your position

Meals and/or lodging (furnished on ministry premises)

Staff Achievement Awards

Final Checklist to Look at Before Finishing and Mailing Your Tax Return:
1999 Income Tax Return Checklist

- ❏ Make a new file folder in which to keep your 1999 tax return and records.
- ❏ Make a copy of your completed federal (and state) return(s), including all attachments, and a file copy of your W-2.
- ❏ Are your filing status and dependents shown correctly on your return?
- ❏ Is your personal information shown correctly on your return?
- ❏ Do all the supporting schedules attached to your return tie in to the proper line on the Form 1040 (the first page of your return)?
- ❏ Is there any refund from 1998 that should carry over and be applied to this year's taxes from last year?
  $ _____
- ❏ Is there any refund that should carry over from 1999 and be applied to next year's taxes from this year?
  $ _____
- ❏ Have you made a comparison of your 1999 return, that you've just completed, to your 1998 return (from last year), to see if there are any unusual year-to-year changes in income, deductions or other items? If there are any unusual year-to-year changes, you'll want to examine these items for possible errors.
- ❏ 1040-ES (if filled out)—these are your estimated tax payments if you're not on voluntary withholding.
- ❏ Do you have any questions about your return to which you can't find the answer? If so, please call IRS help line: 1-800-829-1040. Then curl up in your favorite chair with a good book and wait for them to answer the phone.
- ❏ Are there copies of forms or schedules from your federal return that need to be attached to your state tax return? (Some states require you to attach certain federal forms or schedules to your state return for their information.)

Finalize and Mail Your Return

- ❏ Sign your return and date it. If you're married, your spouse needs to sign and date the return as well.
- ❏ Staple your W-2(s) to the front of your return. (You don't need to attach 1099s to your return, *unless* a 1099 shows Federal Income Tax withheld on line 4 of the 1099.)
- ❏ Staple a check to the front of your return if you owe any tax. Make the check payable to the *United States Treasury*.

Very Important: If you can't pay the tax you owe with your return, **file your return anyway**. This can help stop some penalties from accruing. If you can pay some of the tax you owe when you file your return, this will help stop other penalties from accruing. After you file your return, you may have up to 60 days before the IRS computer gets around to billing you for the balance you owe. Send them a check for whatever you can at that time. They often keep sending bills for up to 90 days more before they begin taking serious enforcement actions. If you keep paying on your tax bill every time you get an IRS notice, you may be able to pay it off before something bad happens.

➡ Tip: If you still can't pay the tax due, file Form 9465 to request installment payments. You can also file this form with your tax return if you wish.

- ❏ If you want to have proof of the date you sent your return to the IRS, the only proof of mailing the IRS will accept is one of the following:
  - U.S. Post Office Certified Mail (use Return Receipt Requested service)
  - Airborne Express—Overnight Air Express Service, Next Afternoon Service and Second Day Service
  - DHL Worldwide Express—DHL Same Day Service and DHL USA Overnight
  - Federal Express—FedEx Priority Overnight, FedEx Standard Overnight and FedEx 2Day
  - United Parcel Service—UPS Next Day Air, UPS Next Day Air Saver, UPS 2nd Day Air and UPS 2nd Day Air A.M.

(If your return is fairly thick because you have a lot of schedules and attachments, use a 9″x12″ manila envelope so you won't have to fold the return.)

Sample Tax Forms

Form **1040**

Department of the Treasury—Internal Revenue Service
U.S. Individual Income Tax Return 1999   (99)   IRS Use Only—Do not write or staple in this space.

For the year Jan. 1–Dec. 31, 1999, or other tax year beginning _____ , 1999, ending _____ , 19 ___ | OMB No. 1545-0074

Label (See instructions on page 12.)

Use the IRS label. Otherwise, please print or type.

LABEL HERE

Your first name and initial | Last name | Your social security number

If a joint return, spouse's first name and initial | Last name | Spouse's social security number

Home address (number and street). If you have a P.O. box, see page 12. | Apt. no.

City, town or post office, state, and ZIP code. If you have a foreign address, see page 12.

▲ **IMPORTANT!** ▲ You **must** enter your SSN(s) above.

Presidential Election Campaign (See page 12.)

Do you want $3 to go to this fund? ....
If a joint return, does your spouse want $3 to go to this fund? ....

Yes | No | Note: Checking "Yes" will not change your tax or reduce your refund.

Filing Status

Check only one box.

1 ☐ Single
2 ☐ Married filing joint return (even if only one had income)
3 ☐ Married filing separate return. Enter spouse's social security no. above and full name here. ▶
4 ☐ Head of household (with qualifying person). (See page 12.) If the qualifying person is a child but not your dependent, enter this child's name here. ▶
5 ☐ Qualifying widow(er) with dependent child (year spouse died ▶ 19___). (See page 12.)

Exemptions

6a ☐ Yourself. If your parent (or someone else) can claim you as a dependent on his or her tax return, **do not** check box 6a
b ☐ Spouse
c Dependents:

(1) First name Last name | (2) Dependent's social security number | (3) Dependent's relationship to you | (4) ✓ if qualifying child for child tax credit (see page 13)

If more than six dependents, see page 13.

d Total number of exemptions claimed ....

No. of boxes checked on 6a and 6b ___
No. of your children on 6c who:
• lived with you ___
• did not live with you due to divorce or separation (see page 13) ___
Dependents on 6c not entered above ___
Add numbers entered on lines above ▶ ___

Income

Attach Copy B of your Forms W-2, W-2G, and 1099-R here.

If you did not get a W-2, see page 14.

Enclose but do not attach any payment. Also, please use **Form 1040-V.**

7 Wages, salaries, tips, etc. Attach Form(s) W-2 . | 7
8a **Taxable** interest. Attach Schedule B if required . | 8a
b **Tax-exempt** interest. DO NOT include on line 8a . 8b
9 Ordinary dividends. Attach Schedule B if required . | 9
10 Taxable refunds, credits, or offsets of state and local income taxes (see page 15) . | 10
11 Alimony received . | 11
12 Business income or (loss). Attach Schedule C or C-EZ . | 12
13 Capital gain or (loss). Attach Schedule D . | 13
14 Other gains or (losses). Attach Form 4797 . | 14
15a Total IRA distributions . 15a ___ b Taxable amount (see page 16) | 15b
16a Total pensions and annuities 16a ___ b Taxable amount (see page 16) | 16b
17 Rental real estate, royalties, partnerships, S corporations, trusts, etc. Attach Schedule E | 17
18 Farm income or (loss). Attach Schedule F . | 18
19 Unemployment compensation . | 19
20a Social security benefits . 20a ___ b Taxable amount (see page 18) | 20b
21 Other income. List type and amount—see page 18 .... | 21
22 Add the amounts in the far right column for lines 7 through 21. This is your **total income** ▶ | 22

[Box 1 and Box 2] [Box 4] [Box 5] [Box 3 + 1099 Income]

Adjusted Gross Income

If line 33 is under $30,095 (under $10,030 if a child did not live with you), see EIC inst. on page 30.

23 IRA deduction (see page 19) . 23
24 Student loan interest deduction (see page 21) . 24
25 Medical savings account deduction. Attach Form 8853 . 25
26 Moving expenses. Attach Form 3903 . 26
27 One-half of self-employment tax. Attach Schedule SE . 27
28 Self-employed health insurance deduction (see page 22) 28
29 Keogh and self-employed SEP and SIMPLE plans . 29
30 Penalty on early withdrawal of savings . 30
31a Alimony paid b Recipient's SSN ▶ _____ 31a
32 Add lines 23 through 31a . | 32
33 Subtract line 32 from line 22. This is your **adjusted gross income** . ▶ | 33

For Privacy Act and Paperwork Reduction Act Notice, see page 52.   Cat. No. 11320B   Form **1040** (1998)

Form 1040 (1998)　　　　　　　　　　　　　　　　　　　　　　　　　　　　　　　　　　Page **2**

Tax and Credits	34	Amount from line 33 (adjusted gross income)	34
	35a	Check if: ☐ **You** were 65 or older, ☐ Blind; **Spouse** was 65 or older, ☐ Blind. Add the number of boxes checked above and enter the total here . . . ▶ **35a**	
	b	If you are married filing separately and your spouse itemizes deductions or you were a dual-status alien, see page 23 and check here . . . ▶ **35b** ☐	
Standard Deduction for Most People	36	Enter the **larger** of your **itemized deductions** from Schedule A, line 28, **OR standard deduction** shown on the left. **But** see page 23 to find your standard deduction if you checked any box on line 35a or 35b **or** if someone can claim you as a dependent	36
Single: $4,250	37	Subtract line 36 from line 34	37
Head of household: $6,250	38	If line 34 is $93,400 or less, multiply $2,700 by the total number of exemptions claimed on line 6d. If line 34 is over $93,400, see the worksheet on page 24 for the amount to enter	38
Married filing jointly or Qualifying widow(er): $7,100	39	**Taxable income.** Subtract line 38 from line 37. If line 38 is more than line 37, enter -0-	39
	40	**Tax.** See page 24. Check if any tax from a ☐ Form(s) 8814 **b** ☐ Form 4972	40
	41	Credit for child and dependent care expenses. Attach Form 2441	41	
Married filing separately: $3,550	42	Credit for the elderly or the disabled. Attach Schedule R	42	
	43	Child tax credit (see page 25)	43	
	44	Education credits. Attach Form 8863	44	
	45	Adoption credit. Attach Form 8839	45	
	46	Foreign tax credit. Attach Form 1116 if required	46	
	47	Other. Check if from **a** ☐ Form 3800 **b** ☐ Form 8396 **c** ☐ Form 8801 **d** ☐ Form (specify)	47	
	48	Add lines 41 through 47. These are your **total credits** . . . . ▶	48
	49	Subtract line 48 from line 40. If line 48 is more than line 40, enter -0- . . ▶	49
Other Taxes	50	Self-employment tax. Attach Schedule SE ⟶ Exempt - Form 4361	50
	51	Alternative minimum tax. Attach Form 6251	51
	52	Social security and Medicare tax on tip income not reported to employer. Attach Form 4137	52
	53	Tax on IRAs, other retirement plans, and MSAs. Attach Form 5329 if required	53
	54	Advance earned income credit payments from Form(s) W-2	54
	55	Household employment taxes. Attach Schedule H	55
	56	Add lines 49 through 55. This is your **total tax** . . . . . . ▶	56

[Diagonal watermark: "Proof as of 5/21/1999"]

[Box at right:] **If you're Social Security exempt, put this here.**

Payments	57	Federal income tax withheld from Forms W-2 and 1099	57	
	58	1999 estimated tax payments and amount applied from 1998 return	58	
Attach Forms W-2 and W-2G on the front. Also attach Form 1099-R if tax was withheld.	59a	**Earned income credit.** Attach Schedule EIC if you have a qualifying child **b** Nontaxable earned income: amount ▶ and type ▶	59a	
	60	Additional child tax credit. Attach Form 8812	60	
	61	Amount paid with Form 4868 (request for extension)	61	
	62	Excess social security and RRTA tax withheld (see page 37)	62	
	63	Other payments. Check if from **a** ☐ Form 2439 **b** ☐ Form 4136	63	
	64	Add lines 57, 58, 59a, and 60 through 63. These are your **total payments** . . . . ▶	64
Refund	65	If line 64 is more than line 56, subtract line 56 from line 64. This is the amount you **OVERPAID**	65
Have it directly deposited! See page 37 and fill in 66b, 66c, and 66d.	66a	Amount of line 65 you want **REFUNDED TO YOU** . . . . ▶	66a
	▶ b	Routing number	
	▶	▶ **c** Type: ☐ Checking ☐ Savings	
	▶ d	Account number	
	67	Amount of line 65 you want **APPLIED TO YOUR 2000 ESTIMATED TAX** ▶	67	
Amount You Owe	68	If line 56 is more than line 64, subtract line 64 from line 56. This is the **AMOUNT YOU OWE**. For details on how to pay, see page 38 . . . . . . ▶	68
	69	Estimated tax penalty. Also include on line 68	69	

Sign Here Keep a copy of this return for your records.	Under penalties of perjury, I declare that I have examined this return and accompanying schedules and statements, and to the best of my knowledge and belief, they are true, correct, and complete. Declaration of preparer (other than taxpayer) is based on all information of which preparer has any knowledge.

Your signature	Date	Your occupation
Spouse's signature. If a joint return, BOTH must sign.	Date	Spouse's occupation

Paid Preparer's Use Only	Preparer's signature ▶	Date	Check if self-employed ☐	Preparer's social security no.
	Firm's name (or yours if self-employed) and address ▶		EIN	
			ZIP code	

SCHEDULES A&B
(Form 1040)

Department of the Treasury
Internal Revenue Service

Schedule A—Itemized Deductions

(Schedule B is on back)

▶ Attach to Form 1040. ▶ See Instructions for Schedules A and B (Form 1040).

OMB No. 1545-0074

19 97

Attachment
Sequence No. **07**

Name(s) shown on Form 1040

Your social security number

					Box 8
Medical and Dental Expenses		Caution: *Do not include expenses reimbursed or paid by others.*			
	1	Medical and dental expenses (see page A-1)	1		
	2	Enter amount from Form 1040, line 33 . [2]			
	3	Multiply line 2 above by 7.5% (.075)	3		
	4	Subtract line 3 from line 1. If line 3 is more than line 1, enter -0-	4		Box 9C
Taxes You Paid (See page A-1.)	5	State and local income taxes	5		
	6	Real estate taxes (see page A-2)	6		Box 9A
	7	Personal property taxes	7		Box 9B
	8	Other taxes. List type and amount ▶	8		
	9	Add lines 5 through 8	9		Box 10
Interest You Paid (See page A-2.)	10	Home mortgage interest and points reported to you on Form 1098	10		
	11	Home mortgage interest not reported to you on Form 1098. If paid to the person from whom you bought the home, see page A-3 and show that person's name, identifying no., and address ▶			
Note: Personal interest is not deductible.			11		
	12	Points not reported to you on Form 1098. See page A-3 for special rules	12		
	13	Investment interest. Attach Form 4952, if required. (See page A-3.)	13		
	14	Add lines 10 through 13	14		Box 12 A, C
Gifts to Charity If you made a gift and got a benefit for it, see page A-3.	15	Gifts by cash or check. If you made any gift of $250 or more, see page A-3	15		
	16	Other than by cash or check. If any gift of $250 or more, see page A-3. You **MUST** attach Form 8283 if over $500	16		Box 12D
	17	Carryover from prior year	17		
	18	Add lines 15 through 17	18		
Casualty and Theft Losses	19	Casualty or theft loss(es). Attach Form 4684. (See page A-4.)	19		
Job Expenses and Most Other Miscellaneous Deductions (See page A-5 for expenses to deduct here.)	20	Unreimbursed employee expenses—job travel, union dues, job education, etc. You **MUST** attach Form 2106 or 2106-EZ if required. (See page A-4.) ▶	20		
	21	Tax preparation fees	21		
	22	Other expenses—investment, safe deposit box, etc. List type and amount ▶	22		
	23	Add lines 20 through 22	23		
	24	Enter amount from Form 1040, line 33 [24]			
	25	Multiply line 24 above by 2% (.02)	25		
	26	Subtract line 25 from line 23. If line 25 is more than line 23, enter -0-	26		
Other Miscellaneous Deductions	27	Other—from list on page A-5. List type and amount ▶	27		
Total Itemized Deductions	28	Is Form 1040, line 33, over $121,200 (over $60,600 if married filing separately)? **NO.** Your deduction is not limited. Add the amounts in the far right column for lines 4 through 27. Also, enter on Form 1040, line 35, the **larger** of this amount or your standard deduction. **YES.** Your deduction may be limited. See page A-5 for the amount to enter. ▶	28		

For Paperwork Reduction Act Notice, see Form 1040 instructions.   Cat. No. 11330X   **Schedule A (Form 1040) 1997**

Schedules A&B (Form 1040) 1997   OMB No. 1545-0074   Page **2**

Name(s) shown on Form 1040. Do not enter name and social security number if shown on other side.	Your social security number

Schedule B—Interest and Dividend Income

Attachment Sequence No. **08**

**Part I
Interest
Income**

(See pages 13 and B-1.)

Note: If you received a Form 1099-INT, Form 1099-OID, or substitute statement from a brokerage firm, list the firm's name as the payer and enter the total interest shown on that form.

Note: *If you had over $400 in taxable interest income, you must also complete Part III.*

		Amount	
1	List name of payer. If any interest is from a seller-financed mortgage and the buyer used the property as a personal residence, see page B-1 and list this interest first. Also, show that buyer's social security number and address ▶		

1

2	Add the amounts on line 1	**2**	
3	Excludable interest on series EE U.S. savings bonds issued after 1989 from Form 8815, line 14. You MUST attach Form 8815 to Form 1040	**3**	
4	Subtract line 3 from line 2. Enter the result here and on Form 1040, line 8a ▶	**4**	

**Part II
Dividend
Income**

(See pages 13 and B-1.)

Note: If you received a Form 1099-DIV or substitute statement from a brokerage firm, list the firm's name as the payer and enter the total dividends shown on that form.

Note: *If you had over $400 in gross dividends and/or other distributions on stock, you must also complete Part III.*

		Amount	
5	List name of payer. Include gross dividends and/or other distributions on stock here. Any capital gain distributions and nontaxable distributions will be deducted on lines 7 and 8 ▶		

5

6	Add the amounts on line 5	**6**	
7	Capital gain distributions. Enter here and on Schedule D, line 14*	**7**	
8	Nontaxable distributions. (See the inst. for Form 1040, line 9.)	**8**	
9	Add lines 7 and 8	**9**	
10	Subtract line 9 from line 6. Enter the result here and on Form 1040, line 9 . ▶	**10**	

If you don't need Schedule D to report any other gains or losses, see the instructions for Form 1040, line 13, on page 14.

**Part III
Foreign
Accounts
and
Trusts**

(See page B-2.)

		Yes	No
	You must complete this part if you **(a)** had over $400 of interest or dividends; **(b)** had a foreign account; or **(c)** received a distribution from, or were a grantor of, or a transferor to, a foreign trust.		
11a	At any time during 1999, did you have an interest in or a signature or other authority over a financial account in a foreign country, such as a bank account, securities account, or other financial account? See page B-2 for exceptions and filing requirements for Form TD F 90-22.1		
b	If "Yes," enter the name of the foreign country ▶		
12	During 1997, did you receive a distribution from, or were you the grantor of, or transferor to, a foreign trust? If "Yes," you may have to file Form 3520 or 926. See page B-2		

For Paperwork Reduction Act Notice, see Form 1040 instructions.   ✪ *Printed on recycled paper*   Schedule B (Form 1040) 1997

SCHEDULE C
(Form 1040)

Department of the Treasury
Internal Revenue Service

Profit or Loss From Business

(Sole Proprietorship)

▶ Partnerships, joint ventures, etc., must file Form 1065.

▶ Attach to Form 1040 or Form 1041.   ▶ See Instructions for Schedule C (Form 1040).

OMB No. 1545-0074

19**97**

Attachment
Sequence No. **09**

Name of proprietor | Social security number (SSN)

A	Principal business or profession, including product or service (see page C-1)	**B** Enter principal business code (see page C-6) ▶			
C	Business name. If no separate business name, leave blank.	**D** Employer ID number (EIN), if any					

E   Business address (including suite or room no.) ▶ ....
       City, town or post office, state, and ZIP code

F   Accounting method: **(1)** ☐ Cash   **(2)** ☐ Accrual   **(3)** ☐ Other (specify) ▶ ....

G   Did you "materially participate" in the operation of this business during 1997? If "No," see page C-2 for limit on losses.   ☐ Yes   ☐ No

H   If you started or acquired this business during 1997, check here   .   .   .   .   ▶ ☐

Church 1099 (or put church 1099 on line 21 instead) ◀

Part I   Income

1	Gross receipts or sales. **Caution:** If this income was reported to you on Form W-2 and the "Statutory employee" box on that form was checked, see page C-2 and check here . . . . ▶ ☐	**1**	
2	Returns and allowances	**2**	
3	Subtract line 2 from line 1	**3**	
4	Cost of goods sold (from line 42 on page 2)	**4**	
5	**Gross profit.** Subtract line 4 from line 3	**5**	
6	Other income, including Federal and state gasoline or fuel tax credit or refund (see page C-2)	**6**	
7	**Gross income.** Add lines 5 and 6 . . . . ▶	**7**	

Part II   Expenses. Enter expenses for business use of your home **only** on line 30.

8	Advertising	**8**		19 Pension and profit-sharing plans	**19**	
9	Bad debts from sales or services (see page C-3) . .	**9**		20 Rent or lease (see page C-4):		
				a Vehicles, machinery, and equipment .	**20a**	
10	Car and truck expenses (see page C-3)	**10**		**b** Other business property . .	**20b**	
11	Commissions and fees . .	**11**		21 Repairs and maintenance . .	**21**	
12	Depletion	**12**		22 Supplies (not included in Part III) .	**22**	
13	Depreciation and section 179 expense deduction (not included in Part III) (see page C-3) . .	**13**		23 Taxes and licenses . . .	**23**	
				24 Travel, meals, and entertainment:		
				a Travel	**24a**	
14	Employee benefit programs (other than on line 19) . .	**14**		**b** Meals and entertainment .		
15	Insurance (other than health) .	**15**		**c** Enter 50% of line 24b subject to limitations (see page C-4) .		
16	Interest:					
a	Mortgage (paid to banks, etc.) .	**16a**		**d** Subtract line 24c from line 24b	**24d**	
b	Other	**16b**		25 Utilities	**25**	
17	Legal and professional services	**17**		26 Wages (less employment credits) .	**26**	
18	Office expense	**18**		27 Other expenses (from line 48 on page 2)	**27**	

Box 7 (attach schedule) ◀

28	**Total expenses** before expenses for business use of home. Add lines 8 through 27 in columns ▶	**28**	
29	Tentative profit (loss). Subtract line 28 from line 7	**29**	
30	Expenses for business use of your home. Attach **Form 8829**	**30**	
31	**Net profit or (loss).** Subtract line 30 from line 29.		
	• If a profit, enter on **Form 1040, line 12,** and ALSO on **Schedule SE, line 2** (statutory employees, see page C-5). Estates and trusts, enter on Form 1041, line 3.	**31**	
	• If a loss, you MUST go on to line 32.		
32	If you have a loss, check the box that describes your investment in this activity (see page C-5).		
	• If you checked 32a, enter the loss on **Form 1040, line 12,** and ALSO on **Schedule SE, line 2** (statutory employees, see page C-5). Estates and trusts, enter on Form 1041, line 3.	**32a** ☐ All investment is at risk.	
	• If you checked 32b, you MUST attach **Form 6198.**	**32b** ☐ Some investment is not at risk.	

For Paperwork Reduction Act Notice, see Form 1040 instructions.   Cat. No. 11334P   Schedule C (Form 1040) 1997

Schedule C (Form 1040) 1997   Page **2**

Part III   Cost of Goods Sold (see page C-5)

33	Method(s) used to value closing inventory: **a** ☐ Cost **b** ☐ Lower of cost or market **c** ☐ Other (attach explanation)	
34	Was there any change in determining quantities, costs, or valuations between opening and closing inventory? If "Yes," attach explanation . . . . ☐ **Yes** ☐ **No**	
35	Inventory at beginning of year. If different from last year's closing inventory, attach explanation . .	**35**
36	Purchases less cost of items withdrawn for personal use	**36**
37	Cost of labor. Do not include salary paid to yourself	**37**
38	Materials and supplies	**38**
39	Other costs	**39**
40	Add lines 35 through 39	**40**
41	Inventory at end of year	**41**
42	**Cost of goods sold.** Subtract line 41 from line 40. Enter the result here and on page 1, line 4 . .	**42**

Part IV   Information on Your Vehicle. Complete this part **ONLY** if you are claiming car or truck expenses on line 10 and are not required to file Form 4562 for this business. See the instructions for line 13 on page C-3 to find out if you must file.

43   When did you place your vehicle in service for business purposes? (month, day, year) ▶ ..../.............../............. .

44   Of the total number of miles you drove your vehicle during 1997, enter the number of miles you used your vehicle for:

a Business ....   **b** Commuting ....   **c** Other ....

45   Do you (or your spouse) have another vehicle available for personal use? . . . . ☐ **Yes**   ☐ **No**

46   Was your vehicle available for use during off-duty hours? . . . . ☐ **Yes**   ☐ **No**

47a   Do you have evidence to support your deduction? . . . . ☐ **Yes**   ☐ **No**

   b   If "Yes," is the evidence written? . . . . ☐ **Yes**   ☐ **No**

Part V   Other Expenses. List below business expenses not included on lines 8–26 or line 30.

◀ *If you don't use the Worksheet from the ClergyTax book, then list your BOX 7 expenses here.*

....	
....	
....	
....	
....	
....	
....	
....	
....	

If you use the ClergyTax Worksheet, then put the BOX 7 total on Line 27 of Schedule C.

48   **Total other expenses.** Enter here and on page 1, line 27 . . . . **48**

Schedule SE (Form 1040) 1998   Attachment Sequence No. **17**   Page **2**

Name of person with **self-employment** income (as shown on Form 1040)	Social security number of person with **self-employment** income ▶	

➡ Don't use if Social Security Exempt

Section B—Long Schedule SE

Self-Employment Tax

Note: *If your only income subject to self-employment tax is **church employee income**, skip lines 1 through 4b. Enter -0- on line 4c and go to line 5a. Income from services you performed as a minister or a member of a religious order **is not** church employee income. See page SE-1.*

A If you are a minister, member of a religious order, or Christian Science practitioner **and** you filed Form 4361, but you had $400 or more of **other** net earnings from self-employment, check here and continue with Part I . . . . . . ▶ ☐

1	Net farm profit or (loss) from Schedule F, line 36, and farm partnerships, Schedule K-1 (Form 1065), line 15a. **Note:** *Skip this line if you use the farm optional method. See page SE-3.*	**1**	
2	Net profit or (loss) from Schedule C, line 31; Schedule C-EZ, line 3; and Schedule K-1 (Form 1065), line 15a (other than farming). Ministers and members of religious orders, see page SE-1 for amounts to report on this line. See page SE-2 for other income to report. **Note:** *Skip this line if you use the nonfarm optional method. See page SE-3.*	**2**	
3	Combine lines 1 and 2	**3**	
4a	If line 3 is more than zero, multiply line 3 by 92.35% (.9235). Otherwise, enter amount from line 3	**4a**	
b	If you elected one or both of the optional methods, enter the total of lines 15 and 17 here . .	**4b**	
c	Combine lines 4a and 4b. If less than $400, **do not** file this schedule; you do not owe self-employment tax. **Exception.** If less than $400 and you had **church employee income**, enter -0- and continue ▶	**4c**	
5a	Enter your **church employee income** from Form W-2. **Caution:** *See page SE-1 for definition of church employee income*	**5a**		
b	Multiply line 5a by 92.35% (.9235). If less than $100, enter -0-	**5b**	
6	**Net earnings from self-employment.** Add lines 4c and 5b . . .	**6**	
7	Maximum amount of combined wages and self-employment earnings subject to social security tax or the 6.2% portion of the 7.65% railroad retirement (tier 1) tax for 1998	**7**	68,400 00
8a	Total social security wages and tips (total of boxes 3 and 7 on Form(s) W-2) and railroad retirement (tier 1) compensation	**8a**	
b	Unreported tips subject to social security tax (from Form 4137, line 9)	**8b**	
c	Add lines 8a and 8b	**8c**	
9	Subtract line 8c from line 7. If zero or less, enter -0- here and on line 10 and go to line 11 . ▶	**9**	
10	Multiply the **smaller** of line 6 or line 9 by 12.4% (.124) . . .	**10**	
11	Multiply line 6 by 2.9% (.029)	**11**	
12	**Self-employment tax.** Add lines 10 and 11. Enter here and on **Form 1040, line 50**	**12**	
13	Deduction for one-half of self-employment tax. Multiply line 12 by 50% (.5). Enter the result here and on **Form 1040, line 27** . . .	**13**	

Optional Methods To Figure Net Earnings (See page SE-3.)

Farm Optional Method. You may use this method **only** if:
- Your gross farm income[1] was not more than $2,400, **or**
- Your gross farm income[1] was more than $2,400 and your net farm profits[2] were less than $1,733.

14	Maximum income for optional methods	**14**	1,600 00
15	Enter the **smaller** of: two-thirds (2/3) of gross farm income[1] (not less than zero) **or** $1,600. Also, include this amount on line 4b above	**15**	

Nonfarm Optional Method. You may use this method **only** if:
- Your net nonfarm profits[3] were less than $1,733 and also less than 72.189% of your gross nonfarm income,[4] **and**
- You had net earnings from self-employment of at least $400 in 2 of the prior 3 years.

Caution: *You may use this method no more than five times.*

16	Subtract line 15 from line 14	**16**	
17	Enter the **smaller** of: two-thirds (2/3) of gross nonfarm income[4] (not less than zero) **or** the amount on line 16. Also, include this amount on line 4b above	**17**	

[1]From Schedule F, line 11, and Schedule K-1 (Form 1065), line 15b.   [3]From Schedule C, line 31; Schedule C-EZ, line 3; and Schedule K-1 (Form 1065), line 15a.
[2]From Schedule F, line 36, and Schedule K-1 (Form 1065), line 15a.   [4]From Schedule C, line 7; Schedule C-EZ, line 1; and Schedule K-1 (Form 1065), line 15c.

Marginal notes (right column):

Note: EITHER use (1) BOX 6 on Line 6; OR use (2) Lines 1, 2, and 5a; BUT NOT Both. ◀

Minister's expenses BOX 7 negative number. ◀

Line 21 items +Housing +Sch C Line ◀

Box 1 + Box 2

Box 6 ◀

Form 2106

Department of Treasury
Internal Rev. Service (99)

Employee Business Expenses

▶ See separate instructions.

▶ Attach to Form 1040.

OMB No. 1545-0139

1994

Attachment
Sequence No. **54**

Your name	Social security number	Occupation in which expenses were incurred

Part I Employee Business Expenses and Reimbursements

			Column A Other Than Meals and Entertainment	Column B Meals and Entertainment
STEP 1	**Enter Your Expenses**			
1	Vehicle expense from line 22 or line 29	1		
2	Parking fees, tolls, and transportation, including train, bus, etc., that did not involve overnight travel	2		
3	Travel expense while away from home overnight, including lodging, airplane, car rental, etc. Do not include meals and entertainment.	3		
4	Business expenses not included on lines 1 through 3. Do not include meals and entertainment	4		
5	Meals and entertainment expenses (see instructions)	5		
6	Total expenses. In Column A, add lines 1 through 4 and enter the result. In Column B, enter the amount from line 5	6		

◀ Box 7

Note: If you were not reimbursed for any expenses in Step 1, skip line 7 and enter the amount from line 6 on line 8.

STEP 2 Enter Amounts Your Employer Gave You for Expenses Listed in STEP 1

7	Enter amounts your employer gave you that were not reported to you in box 1 of Form W-2. Include any amount reported under code "L" in box 13 of your Form W-2 (see instructions)	7		

STEP 3 Figure Expenses To Deduct on Schedule A (Form 1040)

8	Subtract line 7 from line 6	8		

Note: If both columns of line 8 are zero, stop here. If Column A is less than zero, report the amount as income on Form 1040, line 7

9	In Column A, enter the amount from line 8 (if zero or less, enter -0-). In Column B, multiply the amount on line 8 by 50% (.50)	9		

10	Add the amounts on line 9 of both columns and enter the total here. Also, enter the total on Schedule A (Form 1040), line 20. (Qualified performing artists and individuals with disabilities, see the instructions for special rules on where to enter the total.) . . . . ▶	10

For Paperwork Reduction Act Notice, see instructions.

Form **2106**

H733   **210612**   NTF 6732

Copyright Forms Software Only, 1994 Nelco, Inc. N9421061

Form 2106 (1994)   Page **2**

Part II   Vehicle Expenses (See instructions to find out which sections to complete.)

Section A. — General Information

			(a) Vehicle 1	(b) Vehicle 2
11	Enter the date vehicle was placed in service	11		
12	Total miles vehicle was driven during 1994	12	miles	miles
13	Business miles included on line 12.	13	miles	miles
14	Percent of business use. Divide line 13 by line 12	14	%	%
15	Average daily round trip commuting distance.	15	miles	miles
16	Commuting miles included on line 12.	16	miles	miles
17	Other personal miles. Add lines 13 and 16 and subtract the total from line 12	17	miles	miles

18 Do you (or your spouse) have another vehicle available for personal purposes?. . . . . ☐ Yes ☐ No

19 If your employer provided you with a vehicle, is personal use during off duty hours permitted? . . ☐ Yes   ☐ No   ☐ Not applicable

20 Do you have evidence to support your deduction? . . . . ☐ Yes ☐ No

21 If "Yes," is the evidence written?. . . . . ☐ Yes ☐ No

Section B. — Standard Mileage Rate (Use this section only if you own the vehicle.)

22 Multiply line 13 by 31¢ (.31). Enter the result here and on line 1. (Rural mail carriers, see instructions). **22**

◀ Box 11

For 1999 Tax Year 31¢ (.31)

Section C. — Actual Expenses

			(a) Vehicle 1		(b) Vehicle 2	
23	Gasoline, oil, repairs, vehicle insurance, etc.	23				
24a	Vehicle rentals	24a				
b	Inclusion amount (see instructions) .	24b				
c	Subtract line 24b from line 24a.	24c				
25	Value of employer-provided vehicle (applies only if 100% of annual lease value was included on Form W-2 -- see instructions)	25				
26	Add lines 23, 24c, and 25.	26				
27	Multiply line 26 by the percentage on line 14.	27				
28	Depreciation. Enter amount from line 38 below	28				
29	Add lines 27 and 28. Enter total here and on line 1	29				

Section D. — Depreciation of Vehicles (Use this section only if you own the vehicle.)

			(a) Vehicle 1		(b) Vehicle 2	
30	Enter cost or other basis (see instructions)	30				
31	Enter amount of section 179 deduction (see instructions)	31				
32	Multiply line 30 by line 14 (see instructions if you elected the section 179 deduction)	32				
33	Enter depreciation method and percentage (see instructions)	33				
34	Multiply line 32 by the percentage on line 33 (see instructions)	34				
35	Add lines 31 and 34.	35				
36	Enter the limitation amount from the table in the line 36 instructions.	36				
37	Multiply line 36 by the percentage on line 14.	37				
38	Enter the smaller of line 35 or line 37. Also, enter this amount on line 28 above	38				

H733   210612   NTF 6733
Copyright Forms Software Only, 1994 Nelco, Inc. N9421062

Form 4361
(Rev. February 1997)
Department of the Treasury
Internal Revenue Service

Application for Exemption From Self–Employment Tax for Use by Ministers, Members of Religious Orders and Christian Science Practitioners

OMB No. 1545–0168

File Original and Two Copies

File original and two copies and attach supporting documents. This exemption is granted only if the IRS returns a copy to you marked "approved."

Please type or print

1

John or Jane Minister
123 Anystreet
Yourtown, USA

Social security number
123-45-6789

Telephone number (optional)
805/555-1212

2 Check ONE box:
☐ Christian Science practitioner
☐ Member of religious order not under a vow of poverty
☒ Ordained minister, priest, rabbi
☐ Commissioned or licensed minister (see line 6)

3 Date ordained, licensed, etc. (Attach supporting document. See instructions.)
1/1/97

4 Legal name of ordaining, licensing, or commissioning body or religious order

Organization that ordained you

Address
Their Address
Their Address

Employer identification no.
Their EIN

5 Enter the first 2 years, after the date shown on line 3, that you had net self–employment earnings of $400 or more, any of which came from services as a minister, priest, rabbi, etc.; member of a religious order; or Christian Science practitioner ▶ | 1997 | 1998

6 If you apply for the exemption as a licensed or commissioned minister, and your denomination also ordains ministers, please indicate how your ecclesiastical powers differ from those of an ordained minister of your denomination. Attach a copy of your denomination's bylaws relating to the powers of ordained, commissioned, or licensed ministers.

7 I certify that I am conscientiously opposed to, or because of my religious principles I am opposed to, the acceptance (for services I perform as a minister, member of a religious order not under a vow of poverty, or a Christian Science practitioner) of any public insurance that makes payments in the event of death, disability, old age, or retirement; or that makes payments toward the cost of, or provides services for, medical care. (Public insurance includes insurance systems established by the Social Security Act.)

I certify that as a duly ordained, commissioned, or licensed minister of a church or a member of a religious order not under a vow of poverty, I have informed the ordaining, commissioning, or licensing body of my church or order that I am conscientiously opposed to, or because of religious principles, I am opposed to the acceptance (for services I perform as a minister or as a member of a religious order) of any public insurance that makes payments in the event of death, disability, old age, or retirement; or that makes payments toward the cost of, or provides services for, medical care, including the benefits of any insurance system established by the Social Security Act.

I certify that I did not file an effective waiver certificate (Form 2031) electing social security coverage on earnings as a minister, member of a religious order not under a vow of poverty, or a Christian Science practitioner.

I request to be exempted from paying self–employment tax on my earnings from services as a minister, member of a religious order not under a vow of poverty, or a Christian Science practitioner, under section 1402(e) of the Internal Revenue Code. I understand that the exemption, if granted, will apply only to these earnings. Under penalties of perjury, I declare that I have examined this application and to the best of my knowledge and belief, it is true and correct.

Signature ▶ Sign Here   Date ▶ 1/1/98

Caution: Form 4361 is **not proof** of the right to an exemption from Federal income tax withholding or social security tax, the right to a parsonage allowance exclusion (section 107 of the Internal Revenue Code), assignment by your religious superiors to a particular job, or the exemption or church status of the ordaining, licensing, or commissioning body, or religious order.

For Internal Revenue Service Use

☐ Approved for exemption from self–employment tax on ministerial earnings
☐ Disapproved for exemption from self–employment tax on ministerial earnings

By _____   _____
      (Director's signature)   (Date)

CS1

Form **4361** (Rev. 2-97)

a Control number		OMB No. 1545-0008		

b Employer's identification number	1 Wages, tips, other compensation	2 Federal income tax withheld

Box 1 goes here

c Employer's name, address, and ZIP code	3 Social security wages	4 Social security tax withheld
	5 Medicare wages and tips	6 Medicare tax withheld
	7 Social security tips	8 Allocated tips

d Employee's social security number	9 Advance EIC payment	10 Dependent care benefits

e Employee's name, address, and ZIP code	11 Nonqualified plans	12 Benefits included in box 1
	13	14 Other

15 Statutory employee ☐	Deceased ☐	Pension plan ☐	Legal rep. ☐	942 emp. ☐	Subtotal ☐	Deferred compensation ☐

Goes on Schedule A Line 5

16 State	Employer's state I.D. No.	17 State wages, tips, etc.	18 State income tax	19 Locality name	20 Local wages, tips, etc.	21 Local income tax

Department of the Treasury—Internal Revenue Service

Goes on Schedule A Line 5

Form **W-2** **Wage and Tax Statement** **1997**

Copy 2 To Be Filed With Employee's State, City, or Local Income Tax Return

Sample Only (subject to change)

Appendix 1
IRS Says Churches and Other Exempt Organizations Can Look Forward to Heightened Visibility

New Law Changes Every Minister Must Know About

Churches and other exempt organization issues will soon be the subject of increased visibility by the IRS. The general U.S. public will have greater access to confidential church information than ever before in history, according to the IRS.

The IRS is currently undergoing a sweeping reorganization into four new divisions. Under the newly reorganized IRS, one entire division, the new Tax Exempt & Governmental Entities Operating Division, will concentrate on exempt organizations, including churches.

Says a top IRS official in the exempt area: "Starting October 1 you'll have a different IRS to deal with."

New Public Disclosure Rules That Apply to Churches

Currently churches have to make their exemption applications and three most recent information returns available to the public at the church's offices during normal business hours.

Beginning June 8, 1999, there is a new requirement that churches must mail (1) their exemption applications and (2) three most recent information returns to anyone who requests them in writing.

- Churches must now fulfill requests for public disclosure of specific documents by providing copies of the documents without charge, except for reasonable reproduction and postage costs. (A church does not have to accept personal checks for these costs.)
- Documents that must be disclosed include Form 1023, along with any supporting documents filed by or on behalf of the church in connection with an exemption application.
- If the exempt is a religious organization that is not a church, then the three most recent annual information returns (Forms 990, 990-EZ, 990- BL, and Form 1065) must also be disclosed, along with all schedules and attachments filed with the IRS.
- A church is not required to disclose Form 990-T or any parts of an information return that identify names and addresses of contributors. (Churches file this form only if they have unrelated business income.)
- A church that filed its application for exemption before July 15, 1987, is not required to make those applications available, unless the church possessed a copy of the application on July 15, 1987.
- Disclosure of an application for exemption is required only after the IRS has granted an organization exempt status.
- In a change from the proposed regs, the final regs eliminate the requirement that religious or apostolic organizations described in section 501(d) must disclose their Schedules K-1. These are organizations such as religious orders.

- The IRS did not exempt from disclosure compensation information included on an application for exemption or information return.
- A provision permits a principal, regional or district office of an organization to use an agent to process requests for copies.
- Someone who wants to see only part of a Form 1023 or 990 can specifically identify the part or schedule of the document.
- Complaints regarding harassment campaigns against churches should be sent to IRS district directors.
- With regard to the "widely available" option, the final regs do not enumerate any particular computer format that must be used in posting forms on the World Wide Web. The final regs also state that the IRS may issue further guidance to prescribe additional methods that churches may use to make their forms widely available.

Unfortunately, the new IRS Regulations did not specifically exempt churches from providing copies of their exemption application forms (1023s).

This means that effective June 8, 1999 investigative reporters, donors and curious neighbors get free access to the documents filed by the church to gain exempt status.

Here's what any member of the public can now get from a church, under the new rules:
- Articles;
- Bylaws;
- Financial information as of the date the 1023 was filed, including:
     compensation figures;
     income;
     expenses by category;
     balance sheet listing assets and liabilities;
- Various miscellaneous information.

There are those in Washington who read the new rules to mean that *current financial information* must be provided by churches. Certain groups in Washington are working to clarify the law to specifically state this. However, at the time we went to press, there is nothing in the IRS Regulations that would require this interpretation (see the actual language of the new regulations later in this appendix).

The only current alternative for churches to avoid having to mail their documents is if the documents are posted on the Internet—not a very attractive alternative.

The IRS even has an official form that the public can use to request disclosure of documents.

These new rules, according to the IRS, are designed to put churches and other exempts in a "glass house, financially and operationally."

The salaries of top church officers, if contained in the documents filed to get exempt church status, are not exempt from disclosure.

Congressional oversight of churches and other exempts is likely to increase. An IRS spokesman recently said: "The exempt sector represents a significant chunk of the economy outside the tax system, having grown exponentially in the past 20 years."

Some in Washington believe the day is not too far away when Congress may take another look at the whole rationale behind tax exemptions. Because of the enormous cash flows found in the exempt sector (church income nationally is in the billions), Congress may be tempted to look there for more tax revenue.

Already during 1999, a tax bill has been floated that would tax the investment income of some exempt organizations.

Religious organizations that are not churches will be included on CD-ROM releases by the IRS, expected out in the fall of 1999. The CD-ROMs will contain the Form 990 that non-church religious organizations have to file.

Appendix 2
How to Handle 1099s:
Rules for Ministers on 1099s

For ministers on a 1099, start by filling out the Box 1 W-2 Income Worksheet in Part 1. Then, add to that number the following:

If you as a minister get a 1099 instead of a W-2, then health insurance premiums paid for you by the church go in Box 1.

Write the amount here: $ _____.

If you as a minister get a 1099 instead of a W-2, then health expense reimbursements, including payment of insurance deductibles, co-insurance amounts, and any other out-of-pocket expenses paid for you by the church go in Box 1.

Write the amount here: $ _____.

Enter the amount of these items on Schedule C, line 1.

Only those who get a W-2 escape taxation on church-provided health plans. (I don't care what your accountant told you.)

The three major exceptions to the rule that ministers on 1099s don't get fringe benefits are for (1) the 403(b) church retirement plan (due to a recent tax law change), (2) the child care benefit (3) and employer-provided education assistance. And even on these, not everyone agrees that a 1099 minister can get these benefits tax free.

➡ Although the IRS recently took the position that church retirement plans are not available to ministers on 1099s on a tax-free basis, a new law has overruled that position (see appendix 10). The general rule is: It is better to get a W-2 in order to enjoy tax-free fringe benefits.

If you get a 1099, here's what else goes in Box 1:

• Offerings and honorariums to you as a guest speaker, where your offering check is made out to "John Smith." (Sometimes a church where you spoke will ask you to fill out a W-9; this is so they have your Social Security number to put on the 1099.)

Enter the amount of these items on Schedule C, line 1.

If you get a 1099, here's what *doesn't* go in Box 1:

• Offerings and honorariums to you as a guest speaker, where the check is made out to "John Smith Ministries, Inc." or to your church.

• Offerings and honorariums to you as a guest speaker, where check is made out to "John Smith," but the amount is designated as housing allowance for Rev. John Smith (this can be done on the check itself), as long as you actually spent the money on housing items.

Other than these few differences, just go through the part 1 section of *ClergyTax®* to finish your return. Except, in part 1, Box 7, Minister's Professional Expenses are entered on Schedule C. Box 11, business auto expenses are entered on Schedule C, line 10.

Instructions for 1099 Ministers Who Have Business Expenses That Have Not Been Reimbursed by the Church and Who Receive a Housing Allowance

The situation described is commonly known as the Deason rule, or the Dalan rule.

I personally don't agree with this rule for technical reasons, because housing allowance paid to a minister, must, by definition, be spent only on housing-related items to be excludable. Thus, it follows that all expenditures for ordinary and necessary business expenses have to have been made out of ordinary income, and should therefore be deductible. Business expenses of a minister, cannot, by the very nature of the housing allowance itself, be attributable to earning income that is exempt from tax.

However, it is my duty to inform you that if (1) you as a minister receive a 1099 (or no form of any kind at all), (2) you get a housing allowance and (3) you have church-related business expenses that you paid for out of your own pocket and for which the church has not reimbursed you, the IRS is going to take the position that this rule applies to you.

Here's what the rule says in simple terms: The IRS will reduce the amount of business expenses you can deduct by the percentage of your income that is housing allowance.

Here's how it works:

Let's say your housing allowance is $10,000 (this could be what was paid to you, or it can also be the value of a parsonage that the church owned and you lived in).

Let's say your salary is $40,000.

The IRS will divide your $10,000 housing allowance by your $50,000 compensation (salary plus housing), and come up with a percentage of 20. This means they will disallow 20 percent of your business expense deductions under this rule.

So in the previous example, if you have $5,000 of business expenses that you were going to deduct on your Schedule C, current law says you have to reduce that $5,000 by 20 percent. That totals $1,000, and only leaves you with $4,000 of expenses that you can actually deduct.

For many ministers, that means you will pay $300 more in taxes than you would have if you had gotten a W-2 and the church had simply reimbursed you for your business expenses.

Want a perfectly legal tax loophole to get out of the Deason rule?

Here it is: Obtain a W-2 and have your church set up an accountable reimbursement policy (sample minutes are included in this book as appendix 7). This way, when the church reimburses you for church-related expenses, they don't show up on your W-2, and the Deason rule doesn't apply to you at all. All perfectly legal, tax smart, and fully IRS approved.

Appendix 3
Components of a
Minister's Pay Package

You only need to remember three components to set up the best compensation package for a pastor:

1. Fringe benefits—Nontaxable;
2. Fringe benefits—Taxable (covered in part 1 of this book);
3. Salary (covered in part 1 of this book).

How to Handle Fringe Benefits

The following rules are currently the best information on what the IRS will accept on an audit of a minister's personal tax return. We update these rules each year as new information becomes available. In appendix 8, you will find a table showing the tax treatment of fringe benefits for ministers.

Something to Keep in Mind....

If the IRS wants to say that some of your compensation as a minister is excessive, it often will zero in on correct documentation of benefits.

If the IRS looks at your compensation as a minister, it is not a church audit. It is nearly impossible for the IRS to audit a church in this country, even if they were interested in doing so. On the other hand, it is very easy to audit a minister individually.

Common areas where documentation is incomplete or lacking are: retirement plan contributions, fringe benefits, and access to church credit cards.

Be sure your church minutes are up to date.

Fringe Benefit Notes

You want to be sure the fringe benefits you receive are carefully recorded in your church minutes book. While there are many kinds of tax-free fringe benefits, some of the more important ones in terms of dollars are:

- Housing allowance;
- Auto allowance;
- Retirement benefits;
- Paid health insurance (including reimbursement of out-of-pocket expenses);
- Payment of your taxes by the church (this is a taxable fringe benefit).

Housing Allowance

Minister's Housing Allowance

Still the granddaddy of all church benefits, the housing allowance covers essentially your actual expenses regarding your home. Everything from rent or mortgage to cable TV and firewood. Landscaping and even cleaning supplies can be included. (See appendix 5 for more details.)

In some cases, your church can build a home for you and then sell it you. (If they give it to you outright, there will be income in the amount of the value of the equity in the home.)

In most cases, however, I recommend that you buy the home yourself (although the church can provide the down payment), and then pay for it with the housing allowance.

Basically all housing related expenses (subject to certain limits), other than food, clothes, domestic labor and personal toiletry items can be paid for by the church and excluded from income tax. Social Security tax is still due unless you are exempt.

How to Set It Up

You need church minutes each year (preferably in early January or late December) stating the exact amount of the housing allowance for the upcoming year.

Always overdesignate. Any excess you don't use for housing costs will be regular salary, which it would have been anyway.

While not legally required, I like to have two checks written: one for salary, and the other for housing. This proves the exact amount paid for housing.

Keep a folder where you put all your housing-related receipts and checks during the year. At the end of the year you have proof of what you spent.

Is your housing allowance more than 15% to 20% of the value of your home? If yes, review the rules in appendix 5 on Fair Rental Value (FRV) to be sure you're within the guidelines.

What if you're not Social Security exempt and you haven't been paying Social Security tax on your housing allowance? Don't panic! Just make this change with this year's tax return. You may be wondering what happens if you get audited. Generally, if you have made this mistake innocently, the IRS can only go back three years, so it's not the end of the world. And the IRS isn't going to send an innocent person to jail, even if you have made mistakes. All they'll do is want the tax due, plus penalties and interest. If you can't pay it all at once, they'll often set up a payment plan for you. Just think of it as your IRS Visa card. (You even build up travel credits—if you miss a payment, you get a free trip—to the GULAG!)

Do you live in a church-owned parsonage? If so, are you paying Social Security tax (Schedule SE) on the value of your parsonage, if you are not Social Security tax exempt? Social Security tax is due on what the parsonage would rent for if you weren't living in it, plus any utilities the church pays for. Factors such as church use of the parsonage, number of ministers occupying the parsonage, no choice in the matter of the assigned parsonage, etc., may lower the rental value.

A minister can receive a parsonage or housing allowance for only one home.

An additional requirement for purposes of Section 107 is that the fair rental value of the parsonage or parsonage allowance must be reasonable in amount.

Housing allowance must be designated in advance. It cannot be designated retroactively. However, a church can redesignate the housing allowance at any time during the year if needed, effective for the balance of that year. So, for example, if a minister is going to be buying new furniture in August, simply make a redesignation of the housing allowance in July in the church minutes book in the appropriate amount.

The designation may appear in the minister's employment contract, the church minutes, the church budget, or any other document indicating official action. This might include a land contract, deed, or other contract of sale. The designation may also be oral, provided that the church directors certify that the designation was discussed in the context of a church board meeting, however informal. The church may pay a minister's housing expenses directly to the provider, rather than writing a check to the minister.

Example 1

A is an ordained minister. She receives an annual salary of $36,000 and use of a parsonage which has a FRV of $800 a month, including utilities. She has an accountable plan for other business expenses such as travel. A's gross income for arriving at taxable income for federal income tax purposes is $36,000, but for self-employment tax purposes it is $45,600 ($36,000 salary + $9,600 FRV of parsonage).

Example 2

B, an ordained minister, is vice president of academic affairs at Holy Bible Seminary. His compensation package includes a salary of $80,000 per year and a $30,000 housing allowance. His housing costs for the year included mortgage payments of $15,000, utilities of $3,000, and $3,600 for home maintenance and new furniture. The fair rental value of the home, as furnished, is $18,000 per year. The three amounts for comparison are:

1. Actual expenses of $21,600 ($15,000 mortgage payments + $3,000 utilities + $3,600 other costs);
2. Designated housing allowance of $30,000;
3. FRV plus utilities of $21,000 ($18,000 + $3,000 utilities).

B may exclude $21,000 from gross income but must include in income the other $9,000 of the housing allowance. The entire $30,000 will be considered in arriving at net self-employment income.

In the above example, no mention is made of the fair rental value of the furnishings of the home. An examination of the rental value of furniture of the largest furniture rental companies nationwide shows that they use the following computation in renting their furniture: (Cost X 3) ÷ 24. This amount should be added to the fair rental value of the house itself, plus the actual cost of utilities, to arrive at FRV for purposes of the housing exclusion (see above for suggested language).

Example 3

C is an ordained minister and has been employed by his church for the last 20 years. His salary is $40,000 and his designated parsonage allowance is $15,000. C's mortgage was paid off last year. During the tax year he spent $2,000 on utilities, and $3,000 on real estate taxes and insurance. The FRV of his home, as furnished, is $750 a month. The three amounts for comparison are:

1. Actual housing costs of $5,000 ($2,000 utilities + $3,000 taxes and insurance);
2. Designated housing allowance of $15,000;
3. FRV + utilities of $11,000 ($9,000 FRV + $2,000 utilities).

C may only exclude his actual expenses of $5,000 for federal income tax purposes. He may not exclude the FRV of his home even though he has paid for it in previous years. $15,000 will be included in the computation of net self-employment income.

Example 4

Assume the same facts as in Example 3, except that C takes out a home equity loan and uses the proceeds to pay for his daughter's college tuition. The payments are $300 per month. Even though he has a loan secured by his home, the money was not used to "provide a home" and can't be used to compute the excludable portion of the parsonage allowance. The results are the same as for Example 3.

Example 5

D is an ordained minister and received $40,000 in salary plus a designated housing allowance of $12,000. He spent $12,000 on mortgage payments, $2,400 on utilities, and $2,000 on new furniture. The FRV of his home as furnished is $16,000. D's exclusion is limited to $12,000 even though his actual cost ($16,400) and FRV and utilities ($18,400) are more. He may not deduct his housing costs in excess of the designated allowance.

Example 6

E's designated housing allowance is $20,000. She and her husband live in one half of a duplex which they own. The other half is rented. Mortgage payments for the duplex are $1,500 per month. E's utilities run $1,800 per year, and her tenant pays his own from a separate meter. During the year E replaced carpeting throughout the structure at a cost of $6,500 and did minor repairs for $500. E must allocate her mortgage costs, carpeting, and repairs between her own unit and the rental unit in determining the amount of the excludable parsonage allowance. Amounts allocable to the rented portion for mortgage interest, taxes, etc. would be reported on Schedule E as usual. Her actual costs to provide a home were $14,300 ($9,000 mortgage payments, $1,800 utilities and $3,500 for half the carpeting and repairs). The FRV for her unit is the same as the rent she charges for the other half, which is $750 a month, and she estimates that her furnishings add another $150 per month to the FRV. Her FRV plus utilities is $12,600 ($10,800 FRV + $1,800 utilities). E may exclude $12,600 for federal income tax purposes.

Even though a minister's home mortgage interest and real estate taxes have been paid with money excluded from income as a housing allowance, he/she may still claim itemized deductions for these items. The sale of the residence is treated the same as that of other taxpayers, even though it may have been completely purchased with funds excluded under Section 107.

A retired minister may receive part of his/her pension benefits as a designated parsonage allowance based on past services. If so, the "least of" rules apply.

Trustees of a minister's retirement plan may designate a portion of each pension distribution as a parsonage allowance excludable under Section 107. The minister may now claim that the amount is both excludable from income as a parsonage allowance under Section 107 and excludable from self-employment income for Self-Employment Contribution Act (SECA) purposes. Utilities are also covered. This benefit is retroactive, and retired ministers who paid Social Security tax on their housing allowances in 1996, 1997 or 1998 can file amended returns to claim a refund.

Auto Policy

How to Set It Up

You need an auto policy in your church minutes to set up this benefit.

Then title the car in the church name. In some states where this may be difficult, make it clear the auto is owned by the church, even though titled in the minister's name. This strategy is not recommended, but may be necessary due to some state rules.

Who owns your car—you or the church? In almost every case, the church owning the car of the senior minister, along with the correct auto policy in the church minutes, will result in lower taxes each year for the minister, and no additional cost to the church. *Here's why:*

If the church pays the money to the minister, and he or she pays it out for the auto, the money is on the minister's W-2.

On the other hand, if the church pays for the auto directly, rather than paying the minister directly, then the money does not show up on the minister's W-2. Thus, the cost of the auto, including gas, expenses and repairs, escapes both income and Social Security taxes. Then, the only amount that goes on the minister's W-2 is the value of the personal use of the car.

Has your current arrangement been reviewed for (1) legal correctness and (2) for potential tax savings?

Do you have the correct minutes for your church auto policy?

Is personal church auto mileage included on your W-2 each year? You can do this in a few cases by using mileage, but in most cases you will need to use the Annual Lease Value Table for your W-2s each year (see below).

Is the standard mileage rate being used for reimbursements? (31 cents per mile for 1999)

If there are any church autos, is a mileage log kept? This is not a legal requirement, but if you don't have one, you can bet you will be challenged on your mileage by the IRS.

Personal use of a church auto may be determined by the mileage method, but ministers usually have to use the annual lease value method. An auto log or other approved method should be kept to substantiate business mileage. However, some ministers drive each month in substantially the same pattern. If so, a representative log for one month of the year may be sufficient to establish the appropriate business use of a church auto.

Many churches reimburse their ministers for business auto mileage. This is simple and effective (as long as the church has what is known as an "accountable reimbursement plan" in the church minutes). However, I recommend asking the following question—who owns the church auto? It is often tax-wise for the church to own the minister's auto, and include only the personal mileage on the minister's W-2. Possible yearly tax savings: $750 to $1,000.

Church Retirement Plan

Most 403(b) plans for ministers are of the 403(b)(7) type. These are often set up free by insurance companies and mutual funds. There is a reason they are free: While the plan itself is sound, many of the investment vehicles offered by insurance companies and mutual funds would be considered poor by investment experts.

Some church denominations have 403(b)(9) plans, which are more sophisticated and offer more options (often including higher contribution limits) than their (b)(7) cousins. These plans can be set up for independent churches for about $1,200. However, the tremendous benefits you can reap by having such a plan far outweigh the initial paperwork and cost. It may also soon be possible for smaller churches to adopt a standardized form of (b)(9) retirement plan. Stay tuned.

Is a retirement plan currently set up? If not, you're wasting one of the best tax breaks available today for ministers. You can put up to $10,000 per year into one, tax-free (more in certain cases).

Has it been reviewed by a nonprofit tax attorney? You should never attempt to set up a retirement plan yourself. They are very technical.

Is the plan available for staff? Is it paid for staff? You can make payments for other church-staff members, but you don't have to. If the church doesn't make contributions, the staff can make their own contributions out of a salary reduction plan. Do you have a ruling for the plan? You may want to consider having the IRS rule on your plan.

Ministers' Retirement Arrangements

Many churches attempt to set up a "church plan" by merely opening a church bank account. It is this practitioner's experience that many churches in fact set up such "plans," believing them to qualify as retirement plans for their ministers. However, they probably don't qualify under current law. You really need a document that covers the many technical requirements set out in the Code. Congress has recently passed a pension simplification plan just for churches. (Unfortunately, as we go to press, the IRS has not yet released regulations on how this new law will be implemented.)

Comment: There are certain unscrupulous individuals who are selling whole life insurance products to ministers, and claiming that they will qualify as "retirement plans." These individuals claim that premiums paid by the church will not be taxable to the minister (except for the PS 58 cost) because they meet the description of a split dollar plan. They further claim there will be no tax due at distribution, because the "retirement income" comes from loans against the policy buildup. My discussions with the National Office in this regard lead me to believe that the IRS will assert one of two results in these cases:

1. If the minister is audited prior to the retirement plan payouts, the full amount of premiums paid by the church on the minister's behalf will be included in the ministers income for the past three or six years, on the theory that the church never intended a true split dollar arrangement with collateral assignment of the policy, shown by the intent of the parties to allow the minister to have all or substantially all of the policy buildup at a later date.

2. If the minister is audited after the payouts begin, the full amount of policy buildup could be included in the minister's income in the current year, on the theory that the church had transferred the policy buildup to the minister.

Church Health Plan

Medical Expenses. These are tax-free, whether the premiums are paid for or not (sometimes even if your out-of-pocket costs are reimbursed by the church, if insurance has not been purchased). This means the church can pay your medical insurance premiums, and often pay whatever is not covered by the deductible as well.

How to Set It Up
The plan should be in writing, and be in the church minutes.

You'll find sample minutes for a medical expense reimbursement policy in appendix 6 in this edition of *ClergyTax*®.

Other Nontaxable Fringe Benefits

General rule: It's always better to receive a benefit instead of salary, where you were going to pay for the benefit anyway.

1. *Group term life insurance.* Premiums for up to $50,000 of this kind of insurance are tax-free to you. They're usually quite inexpensive also.

How to Set It Up
Just put it in the church minutes, and have your insurance agent set up the plan. Shop around for the best rates.

2. *Disability insurance.* Premiums are tax-free (but benefits are taxable; benefits are tax-free only if you pay the premiums yourself).

How to Set It Up
Again, just put it in the church minutes, and have your insurance agent set up the plan. Look for rates that include permanent payments if these become necessary.

3. *Reimbursements of church expenses.* The church should always reimburse you for the following expenses, all tax-free to you:

- Subscriptions to religious publications;
- The business use of your car (if you own it) at 31 cents per mile;
- Educational expenses related to being a minister or other church-staff job (this can include conferences or seminars);
- Membership and dues in professional associations;
- Seminars, conventions, classes;
- All types of church-related materials and supplies related to your position;
- Anything else related to doing your job as a minister;
- Parking fees up to $175 per month, if you have to pay to park near work.

Do you have an accountable church reimbursement policy? If not, you should. Sample minutes are found in appendix 7.

If not, are you reporting all reimbursements as income on your W-2? With no accountable plan set up, all reimbursements are gross income to you.

4. *Cafeteria plans.* These are benefit packages where the minister or staff member chooses from a menu of benefits which ones they want.

Now, here are some more exotic fringe benefits, which you may not have heard about:

5. *Child-care or dependant benefits.* You can receive up to $5,000 of church-paid child-care or disabled dependent-care services each year. This can be provided at the church daycare facility, or the church can reimburse you for expenses you incur. You have to have a written plan and the amount received can't exceed your earned income from the church (in other words, your salary must at least equal the amount of benefits you receive under this plan).

If your spouse is on staff, the benefits can't exceed the spouse's income. And, if you use the reimbursement variety, you have to set aside money from your salary at the beginning of the year and get reimbursements as you go.

Note: Check with your tax advisor to see if you need to file Form 2441 with your tax return in regard to this benefit.

6. *Education benefits.* The church can pay up to $5,250 of education assistance for you each year. This can include tuition, fees, books and course supplies.

Note: This benefit expired on December 31, 1994, but Congress has extended it again. The current benefit program runs from January 1, 1995 through May 31, 2000. (In the case of graduate courses, the benefit expired after June 30, 1996). ➡This means that ministers can get a refund for taxes, interest and penalties which they paid because they didn't think they could exclude church-paid educational assistance provided in 1996, 1997 and 1998.

Note: Legislation is currently pending that would apply the exclusion for church-provided education assistance, for both graduate and undergraduate education, to courses beginning on or before June 30, 2004.

7. *Legal services.* Your church can probably provide legal services for you to have your income tax return prepared as a business-related expense.

This is because the tax laws are so complex for ministers, and because the church itself must have competent guidance in order to take the steps needed to properly report compensation and benefits to a minister. The more church-related questions are involved, the more likely this benefit will be tax-free to you.

Note: This benefit has never been officially endorsed by the IRS. But current tax law probably allows it, since you can usually deduct this expense on a Schedule C.

8. *On-premises athletic facilities.* This is not likely to apply to a lot of churches, but if your church has a gym, workout room, tennis courts or other sports-related facility, minister or staff use of it is a tax-free fringe benefit.

9.   *De minimis fringe benefits.* This means fringe benefits that aren't worth enough for the government to make you keep a record of them. The only requirement is that they can't be paid in cash—the benefit itself must be provided. Some examples:

   - $65 a month of bus, train or limo "transit pass" fares;
   - Occasional supper money and/or taxi fare when you work overtime;
   - Low value holiday gifts, such as a turkey or ham;
   - Long-distance telephone calls;
   - Picnics and Christmas parties;
   - Occasional tickets to sports events;
   - Free coffee and snacks;
   - Use of the copy machine;
   - Free postage stamps;
   - Use of secretarial services for personal items.

10. *Church cafeteria.* There are a few churches that run a cafeteria or commissary. As long as the church charges you enough to basically just cover the direct costs of running the eatery, the full retail value of the meal is not income to you. You can just buy your meals at cost.

11. *Employee discounts.* You can buy books from the church bookstore for cost. You can pay for services, such as Bible school tuition, at 20% less than what you charge everyone else, with no problems, as long as that is not below the cost to the church.
      This fringe benefit also includes qualified tuition reductions at a Christian school run by a church. This can also apply to staff, and their spouses or dependent children.

12. *No additional cost services.* There aren't going to be many of these for churches. An example would be like an airline giving a big discount to an employee for an empty seat, or a hotel giving an empty room to an employee. (Maybe you could get the staff saved—even if they don't tithe.) Another example: free admission to the New Heritage USA for staff members there (forgive me, Lord).

13. *Meals and/or lodging.* Some ministries furnish meals and/or lodging to their staff because they are located way out in the boondocks. The meals have to be furnished on ministry premises, and the lodging must be required as a condition of employment, for instance because the staff member is on call 24 hours a day.

14. *Holiday gifts.* As mentioned above, holiday turkeys and hams are tax-free, as well as other holiday gifts of nominal value, such as clocks, travel bags, and pens. However, cash and gift certificates are always taxable, regardless of value.

15. *Staff achievement awards.* Did you know you can give awards for length-of-service or safety achievement up to $400? The only catch is that the award cannot be in cash, but must be some type of "tangible personal property." This includes items like watches, gold fountain pens, jewelry, stereos, VCRs, TVs and other such goodies.

And, if you have what is known as a qualified plan, the maximum award can go all the way up to $1,600. You have a qualified plan, as long as the average award is no more than $400. For example, if the church has five people on staff, and three of them get an award in the amounts of $100, $100, and $1,000, then the average award is $400, and the plan is qualified and all three awards are tax-free.

If you think of any other benefits I haven't mentioned, just be creative and include them in your package. Most fringes not mentioned in this section will be taxable. Usually the main requirement is that the benefit be approved in your church minutes.

Here are some brand-new tax-free fringe benefits approved by Congress just recently:

16. *Adoption assistance.* If your church has an adoption assistance program and pays adoption expenses on your behalf, you can exclude from your gross income up to $5,000 ($6,000 for a child with special needs) of these benefits. (However, these amounts are subject to Social Security and Medicare taxes, unless the minister is exempt.) There is also a credit available on the minister's individual tax return. You may be

able to claim a credit of up to $5,000 (or $6,000) and also exclude up to $5,000 (or $6,000) from your income. However, you cannot claim both a credit and an exclusion for the same expense.

17. *IRA withdrawals to pay medical expenses and medical insurance.* You generally pay a 10% penalty if you withdraw funds from your IRA before a certain age. However, you may not have to pay the penalty if the withdrawals are used to pay unreimbursed medical expenses that are more than 7% of your adjusted gross income. (But it's still going to be cheaper from a tax standpoint if the church simply reimburses you for these expenses on a tax-free basis.)

  If a minister loses his or her job, funds may be taken from an IRA without paying the 10% penalty if the withdrawals are not more than the amount paid for medical insurance for the minister and family.

18. *Medical savings accounts.* Certain persons who are covered under a high-deductible health plan may be able to participate in a medical savings account program. You would then be able to deduct up to $1,462.50 ($3,375 for family coverage) per year for contributions to a medical savings account, even if you do not itemize your deductions. Proceeds from this account can be used to pay unreimbursed medical expenses. (Again, it may be better for the church just to reimburse you tax-free for these expenses—check with your tax advisor.)

Fringe Benefit Example

Let's look at an example. Let's say the church wants to buy you a universal life insurance policy, which not only insures your life, but also builds up a savings account for you.

This particular benefit is taxable for both income and Social Security tax purposes.

If the premiums are $500 per month, the church will pay $6,000 a year on your behalf, and this amount will show up on your W-2.

Social Security tax is right at 15%, which would be $900.

If your income-tax bracket is 15% as well, that would be another $900.

So your total cost for a $6,000 benefit is only the $1,800 in extra taxes you'll pay.

To me, that spells b-a-r-g-a-i-n.

MINISTER'S INCOME NOTES

Important Notes

1. Don't go over $100,000 of salary, plus benefits, in your compensation package without an attorney's opinion letter.

2. Don't ever set your salary as a percentage of gross income of the church, or put your name as one of the check-offs on the offering envelope. (However, a new law may, for the very first time, allow some ministers to be paid based on how fast their church grows—so-called "pay for performance"—and have their compensation linked in some way to church revenue. See appendix 9. Caution: The IRS has not yet issued regulations yet on this new possibility. My advice is wait and see what the rules are before jumping in.)

3. Be sure your minutes designate your pay as compensation for ministerial duties, not for sitting on the board (this can help you under many state limited liability rules).

4. Have your church give you a W-2 each year and use voluntary withholding. This will lock in your eligibility for many nontaxable fringe benefits—and lower your chance of an audit at the same time.

5. Have your salary "signed off" by outside directors, if this is possible. If not, be sure you show how you arrived at each item of compensation.

6. You want to be sure the total amount of your compensation is reasonable in your area for the work you do, including hours put in, results achieved, your experience, and the demands of your job.

7. You want to be sure the total amount of your compensation is reasonable in your area for the work you 7. Has your church ever made a loan to you as minister? If yes, were state laws checked? (Some states don't allow this.)

8. Has your personal tax situation been reviewed in connection with how the church handles your salary and benefits? Pay attention to the each of the rules given in *ClergyTax®*, and help eliminate problems.

9. Life insurance policies:

   - Who owns them? (Church paid premiums are probably taxable if you own the policy.)
   - Who pays the premiums? (The church can pay for your insurance as a taxable benefit.)
   - Who is the beneficiary? (If the church is the beneficiary, the premiums aren't taxable to you.)
   - What are the face amounts? (Do you have enough to cover known needs?)
   - Who gets the cash value? (Split dollar plans allocate the cash between the church and the pastor.)

   Is there a key man life insurance policy? If so, the church can pay the premiums, and they won't be taxable to the minister (except to the extent members of the minister's family are cobeneficiaries on the policy).

10. Is disability covered? It should be.

11. Does your church Board:

    - Determine the annual pay of the minister officers and senior church employees?
    - Approve all loans, gifts and benevolence?
    - Make sure all of these are made in accordance with church tax exempt purposes?
    - Follow the church bylaws and articles for meetings, elections, etc.?
    - Designate housing allowances in advance each year?
    - Require receipts to be kept by each minister?

12. Are any teachers in your church school ordained? If so, do these teachers receive a housing allowance? If not, they should be. Have they been informed that they may elect out of Social Security by filing Form 4361?

WHO QUALIFIES FOR SPECIAL TAX TREATMENT AS A MINISTER

In order to qualify for the special tax provisions available to ministers, an individual must be a "minister" and must perform services "in the exercise of his ministry." A "minister" is a duly ordained, commissioned or licensed individual who performs services in the exercise of his or her ministry. Services performed by a minister in the exercise of his or her ministry include the ministration of the sacraments, the conduct of worship services, preaching, the administration and maintenance of religious organizations and their integral agencies, and administrative duties at theological seminaries.

Services considered to be within the exercise of the ministry include performing marriage and funeral services, serving as a university chaplain, teaching or otherwise serving on the faculty at schools operated under the authority of a religious organization, performing church assignments such as writing or charity work, even if performed in conjunction with a nonreligious organization. A minister must be "ordained, licensed, or commissioned" to perform his/her duties; however, religious disciplines vary in their formal procedures for these designations. Even though a minister is an employee, he or she is permitted to use Schedule C to report fees for weddings, funerals, baptisms, and masses and to deduct related expenses.

The five criteria the courts have used for deciding who is a minister are:

A. Ordained, licensed, or commissioned;
B. Lead religious worship;
C. Administer the sacraments;
D. Have administrative or management duties at a church or denomination;
E. Considered to be a spiritual leader within the church.

Having A, along with any two of the other four, is generally considered to indicate that someone is a minister for tax purposes. There are one or two cases that state that all five of the above are required, but the best cases (and now the new IRS Ministers' Audit Guidelines) note that A, together with any two of the other four, will qualify in most cases.

Here's something I learned at a young age: When there's not enough money, as is often the case when we're discussing minister's compensation, there are two things you can do (1) cut expenses, or (2) make more money. The second is always easier, and a lot more fun. Here's a radical suggestion: If you don't have enough money to fully fund a Pastor's compensation the way you want to, simply start an evangelistic outreach program to get 50 or 100 more people in the church. That should more than take care of the shortfall in most situations. If you can't find any more people for the church, than you might as well get used to being as poor as a church mouse.

Missionaries

Contributions made to or for the support of individual missionaries to further the objectives of their missions are includible in gross income.

Many missionaries qualify for the foreign income exclusion. As far as I know, no one has yet addressed the issue of whether support raised by foreign missionaries in the U.S. to be used for their foreign missions objectives can be excluded if the missionary has established bona fide foreign residency. I suggest that it does so qualify, since it is comparable to sending a donation to a foreign charity: not deductible to the U.S. donor, and not reportable by the recipient.

Another issue is whether donations made directly to U.S. based missionaries are fully subject to self-employment taxes. The target of the rule is probably living expenses, but it would seem that amounts expended by the missionary to further genuine missions objectives, should be allowable as an offset on Schedule SE. Again, I know of nothing published which speaks to this issue.

In the case of missionaries with a foreign residence, these contributions may be excluded under the foreign income exclusion to the extent allowable. In the case of U.S. based missionaries, the missionary may deduct expenses related to mission objectives other than basic living expenses on Schedule SE.

In the case of a missionary under the authority of a local church or other missions board, the missionary should account to the missions board for all amounts sent overseas by the board. Any salary, or amounts not accounted for, should be included on a form W-2 issued to the missionary. In the case of donations by individuals directly to a missionary, they are not deductible by the donor as charitable contributions, but may be included in the income of the missionary, unless they are personal gifts from family members.

Audits of Ministers

1. In 1995 the IRS announced a program to conduct detailed audits of ministers. The information was published by Tax Analysts, the highly respected Washington tax publishing group. This program is expected to continue during 1999, 2000 and on into the year 2001. However, now there will be much more at stake: the new "intermediate sanctions" rules (see appendix 9 for an overview, and appendix 10 for more detail) allow the IRS to impose penalties on ministers during audits if the agent thinks the new rules are not being followed correctly.

   Exact audit numbers are never announced—only total audit goals and the groups that are targets of the audits. It is up to practitioners to figure out, based on percent of population estimates, IRS priorities, and other factors, what the official announcement means for a particular group of taxpayers. I have reason to believe, based on my work in this area, past experience, and knowledge of how IRS initiatives develop over time, that the actual number of minister audits will be much greater for particular groups of ministers.

2. The IRS can only go back three years to audit personal tax returns. However, if there is a significant amount of unreported income, or if the IRS feels there is fraud involved, the three-year limit does not apply, and in some cases there is no limit on how far back the IRS can go.

3. While the IRS cannot examine church records except in very extreme circumstances, because of Internal Revenue Code Section 7611, a church can sometimes produce certain minute book records in the situation where a minister is being audited, and shorten the audit by doing so. In my view, there are many audits where it is appropriate to do this, and help out the minister. (There are also some situations where this would be a big mistake—consult your tax attorney before making any church records available to the IRS.)

4. If you as a minister set, or participate in setting, your own salary, have your compensation package "signed off" by outside directors. If your church board or denominational headquarters sets your compensation, be sure they have material in this article handy so they can avoid mistakes that cost you money or get you audited. (See new appendix 9 about the new "Intermediate Sanctions" law and the safe harbor you can take advantage of.)

5. In the course of minister's audits, the situation often arises where personal expenses have been charged on church credit cards, and not reimbursed by the minister, or church expenses have been charged on personal credit cards, without reimbursement from the church. Other types of "sloppy bookkeeping" can also occur. Rather than spend the time going through each and every credit card statement, or through each and every check, a sampling procedure for various items of proof can be adopted. The examiner will choose a month or other time period to be examine, and the taxpayer will prove up the appropriate figures for the periods chosen by the examiner. The results can be applied to the entire year or years under examination. The taxpayer should also have the opportunity to request that additional time periods be added to the sample, in the event that the sample chosen would unfairly penalize the taxpayer because it wasn't representative of the year as a whole, for example, because a single particularly large purchase, or a large number of purchases, were made during that time.

6. It arises during audits of ministers, that the minister has records of business expenses, but has not contemporaneously recorded the business purpose thereof. Rather than just disallow wholesale such expenses, which produces an unfair result (because most ministers are basically honest in their recordkeeping), the examiner can make use of personal testimony of the minister or spouse, comments from church treasurers familiar with various expense items, or methods of indirect proof proffered by the taxpayer.

7. Ministers often receive "expense" accounts and "allowances", which are basically nonaccountable reimbursements. However, often the church board merely intended to reimburse the minister for his or her out-of-pocket expenses related to church business, but did not receive adequate guidance from its tax advisor (if any). In an appropriate case, the examiner may want to take into consideration the actual intent of the church board, however flawed the implementation. Then instructions can be given on how to handle future ministerial reimbursements.

8. Many ministers maintain a home office for sermon preparation, administrative duties, hosting church gatherings, and other church-related duties. The Deason rule would appear to prevent deduction of these home office expenses in most cases. However, travel to and from the home office to the church office may be deductible transportation, much the same as a doctor, or other professional, traveling from a home office to a hospital or clinic.

9. Occasionally a minister may receive no compensation for services. In this case, any actual out-of-pocket costs are deductible as charitable contributions. This would also be true where the minister paid expenses on behalf of a smaller church the income of which was not sufficient to pay same, as long as the expenses were related to the exempt purposes of the church. In either case, these payments could also be considered as deductible business expense.

Here is an actual IRS example of how they would handle your tax return as a minister:

Example 8

G received a salary of $12,000, a housing allowance of $9,000, and earned $3,000 for various speaking engagements, weddings, funerals, etc., all related to her ministry. She reports her salary as wages on page 1 of her Form 1040 and her fees on Schedule C . Because her actual housing costs ($6,000) were less than her housing allowance and the FRV of her home for the year, she must include $3,000 of her housing allowance as other income for income tax purposes. Her total business expenses are $4,500. The computation of deductible expenses is shown below:

$6,000 (housing allowance actually exempt from income tax) _____= 25% Nontaxable
$24,000 ($12,000 salary + $9,000 housing + $3,000 fees) income
Total expenses $4,500 x 25% = $1,125 = Nondeductible expenses
Total expenses $4,500 - $1,125 = $3,375 = Deductible expenses.

Note that this $3,375 would further be allocable between Schedule A miscellaneous deductions (related to salary) and Schedule C (related to other fees). However, as you will see in the next section, this allocation will not change G's self-employment tax, since all ministry income and ministry expenses are included in the computation, regardless of where they are reported on the return for income tax purposes. The allocation between Schedule A and Schedule C will also affect any AGI-dependent computations.

Notes on the 4361 (Social Security Tax) Exemption

There is a recent case, Eade v. United States, 792 F. Supp. 476 (W.D. Va. 1992), stating that IRS approval of a minister's self-employment tax exemption is a ministerial act, where the minister has met all the requirements of the Code. This distinction can be important where the Post Office or the IRS loses the 4361, or it becomes misdirected in some manner.

How do you tell when the time limit begins to run for filing your Social Security tax exemption?

For example, if minister H earns $300 in 1998 from preaching, and has $800 in reimbursements under an accountable plan, he does not have $400 of net self-employment ministerial earnings in that year. Likewise, if minister H earns $1,200 from preaching in 1999, and has $900 of deductible expenses related to his ministry, he does not have $400 of net self-employment ministerial earnings in that year.

The exemption from self employment tax applies only to services performed as a minister. The exemption does not apply to other types of earned income.

Where Form 4361 has been approved, the taxpayer should not file Schedule SE, and should mark on line 47 of the 1040: "Exempt-Form 4361", or "Exempt-F4361". Where Form 4361 has been filed, but the approved copy has not yet been received by the taxpayer, IRS Service Center personnel say the taxpayer should file the tax return without Schedule SE attached, and mark on line 47 of the 1040: "Form 4361 Pending".

Note: You may be able to file for a refund of past Social Security tax paid after you have gotten your 4361 Social Security tax exemption as a minister. See your tax advisor.

A SECOND CHANCE TO ELECT
OUT OF Social Security COVERAGE

A federal court in the 10th Circuit has given some ministers a second chance to elect out of Social Security.

A 1994 federal court case now says that ministers who originally began their ministry and missed the time limit for electing out of Social Security, and who later change churches, can qualify a second time to file Form 4361 and opt out of the Social Security system. Here's what the federal judge said:

"When an individual enters the ministry anew in a new church, having adopted a new set of beliefs about the propriety of accepting public insurance, it is logical and consistent with the statutory language of section 1402(e) to characterize that individual as a "new" minister for the purposes of seeking an exemption. The plain language does not preclude this sensible reading."

"Ministers who do switch will still have a limited time frame in which to file for exemption following their assumption of the duties and functions of the new ministry."

The religious conviction cited by this particular minister as a basis for his opting out was that the minister believed he should "live by faith," and let the Lord supply his needs. The court agreed this religious principle could form the basis for a valid exemption from the Social Security system.

Here's What Happened

The minister in this case was originally ordained as a deacon in a large denomination.

Then, from 1980 to 1983, he served as minister of one of the denomination's churches.

During his tenure as minister, he paid Social Security taxes on his ministerial earnings. His last date to elect out of Social Security coverage was April 15, 1982, the due date of his 1981 return, 1981 being the second year he had ministerial earnings of at least $400 subject to Social Security tax.

Neither the minister nor his denomination at the time were opposed to Social Security coverage.

The minister then left his pastorate, and worked as an engineer for the next five years.

He later returned to the ministry, and was ordained by an independent evangelical church in the Midwest. He also began a new evangelistic ministry that year, based out of Colorado Springs.

The independent church was opposed to Social Security coverage on religious grounds. The church believed the minister should "live by faith," and let the Lord supply his needs. The minister agreed with this religious principle.

So, the minister then filed Form 4361 in a timely manner, based on his ordination with the independent church, and based on his earnings from his evangelistic ministry. The IRS rejected the minister's Form 4361.

The case went to Tax Court, which upheld the IRS. The minister appealed to the 10th Circuit.

The 10th Circuit Court of Appeals decided that when an individual "enters the ministry anew in a new church, having adopted a new set of beliefs... that individual [is] a 'new' minister *for purposes of seeking an exemption*" from *Social Security coverage.*

The Court pointed out that it wasn't going to hurt anything if a small group of ministers wanted to drop out of the Social Security system. The Court thought it was unlikely that a minister would elect out, and give up Social Security benefits, unless they had a legitimate religious conviction.

Commentators on this case have said that most ministers take the position of: "Praise the Lord! but keep those Social Security checks coming."

What Does This Mean for Ministers Today?

1. Change of belief alone is not enough. The court emphasized that:
2. Changing denominations (or churches) is the critical act that gives rise to the new opportunity to elect out of Social Security coverage.
3. Pitfall: It is possible that serving as a minister in a new church or denomination before becoming ordained in that new church or denomination could mark the start of the new time for electing out of Social

Security coverage. In other words, if a minister changed churches or denominations, worked in the new church or denomination for, say, four years before becoming ordained in the new church or denomination, he or she may lose the right to elect out based on the change to a new church or denomination, because the new period began to run when the ministry began at the new church or denomination, instead of later when the new ordination occurred. This fact pattern is in doubt under current law. A minister in this situation, or a minister who has had a change of religious belief even though he or she has not changed churches or denominations, can file Form 4361, along with a Form 4875-R to explain what is being done, quit paying Social Security tax, and then fight any IRS deficiency in court on constitutional grounds. Consult a competent nonprofit tax attorney before attempting this course of action, and expect to be challenged by IRS.

4.   Although the Court did not address this issue: What happens if you don't change churches, but your church changes denominational affiliations? The best advice is probably to go ahead and file a Form 4361 if you are opposed to Social Security coverage because "the Lord will provide." If you wait to file the Form 4361, you might lose your possible new opening to elect exemption.

5.   High earning individuals (more than $60,600) who work as ministers part time don't pay Social Security tax on their church earnings anyway, since amounts greater than $60,600 are above the Social Security tax ceiling. However, such earnings are still subject to Medicare tax of about 3%.

6.   Here's what not to do: Don't even think about taking up offerings for a minister on a regular basis and calling them "love offerings." You could end up facing criminal charges for doing this, since the IRS takes the position that even offerings to a minister are considered income. Also, in a related area, putting the minister's name on the offering envelope can cost your church it's tax exemption, because the IRS takes the position that such income could be unlimited.

7.   If you are a minister (1) who has a conviction against Social Security coverage, and (2) who has changed churches or denominations and (3) has become recently ordained in the new church or denomination, the way is now open for you to file Form 4361 and exempt yourself from Social Security coverage. The Court's position is they don't care, since that's one less person they'll have to make Social Security payments to. That's only partially true, since even if you elect out, you will still receive Social Security payments on all benefits which are "vested" at the time you elect out. "Vesting" usually occurs after you have paid in to Social Security for at least 40 quarters.

Summary

If you have been paid as a minister for the first time on or after January 1, 1998, you have until April 15, 2000 to file Form 4361 and elect out of Social Security. You can extend this date by filing an extension for your 1999 tax return by certified mail, return receipt requested.

Form 4361 is a (deceptively) simple, one-page form. Consult a competent nonprofit tax attorney if you feel you might need help filling it out. A typical fee for such a form is about $100.

If you have already filed Form 4361 and been rejected for a reason you feel is incorrect: see a good attorney immediately. Often the IRS rejects 4361s because a minister has filled out the form incorrectly and doesn't realize that a mistake has been made.

If you filed Form 4361 many years ago and now can't find your approved copy, try writing both the IRS and the Social Security Administration under the Freedom of Information Act and see if you can get a copy of your approved 4361.

Many ministers ask what is sufficient "religious conviction" to opt out of Social Security. To answer that, please keep this in mind: the election out of Social Security is based on your objection to *receiving Social Security benefits* on your earnings as a minister. You can still receive benefits based on the secular earnings you had before you became a minister, or even on secular earnings you have while you act as a minister part-time.

If you believe "the Lord will provide" for your needs, this is a sufficient religious belief. Some ministers quote the verse: "he who preaches the Gospel, shall live by the Gospel." A simple belief that God will take care of your retirement—rather than the government doing it—is enough to qualify for the exemption. And there are church denominations that take the matter further, and feel that it is their religious duty to take care of not only their ministers, but also their church members, in health and retirement matters, so the government doesn't have to. The law protects your religious beliefs at either end of this spectrum, or anywhere in between.

But please know: Once you elect out, that's it. The election is irrevocable, which means you can't reenter the Social Security system at a later time. That's to prevent people from electing out, escaping the tax, then electing back in right before it's time to retire. So, if you elect out, be sure your church makes some provision for your retirement. The IRS has blessed at least two types of generous church retirement plans.

Is it wrong to elect out of Social Security coverage? I can't see how it would be. Your belief that the Lord—perhaps through your own church retirement plan—should take care of you, rather than the government, is enough. The IRS, the Congress, and the Courts all respect a minister's right to make his or her own decision in this area. *James B. Hall*, No. 93-4027, *94 TNT 154-21* (10th Cir. 1994)

Appendix 4
Checklist of Deductions for Ministers

Here is a handy checklist of the most common deductions for ministers so you aren't as likely to miss any:

Minister's Professional Expenses

Auto expenses	$ _____
Educational expenses	$ _____
Books	$ _____
Tapes	$ _____
Other religious materials	$ _____
Office supplies	$ _____
Postage	$ _____
Seminars and dues	$ _____
Subscriptions and fees	$ _____
Office equipment	$ _____
Accounting fees	$ _____
Tax return preparation	$ _____
Post office box	$ _____
Business telephone	$ _____
Interest on charge cards used for business	$ _____
Interest on auto loan(s) for cars used 100 percent for business	$ _____
Interest on other business-related loan(s) (such as credit union, finance company, personal, educational, bank or life insurance loan)	$ _____
Other _____	$ _____

But Keep in Mind

Did the church *reimburse* you for any of these church-related *expenses*?

➡ If no, then deduct only the expenses for which your church has not reimbursed you. If yes, has your church adopted an accountable church reimbursement policy in the minutes? If so, then the church doesn't have to put them on your W-2, and you don't have to deduct them either.

Professional Travel

This includes seminars, conventions and so forth. You can deduct items *not* paid for by the church. It is best to keep a *trip diary* for your records to show the *ministry purpose* of the travel.

Auto rental $ _____
Fares (air, train or bus) $ _____
Hotel $ _____
Laundry and cleaning $ _____
Parking and tolls $ _____
Telephone $ _____
Meals $ _____
Tips $ _____
Other _____ $ _____

➡ *Be sure you have receipts for these travel expenses. The IRS almost always checks these in an audit.*

If you *do* have receipts, please keep them in a file marked "1999 expenses." If *not*, please note for which items receipts are missing. They can still be deducted, but you should know that if your return is audited, they will probably be disallowed unless you kept an *expense diary* during the year. An "expense diary" can be a pocket calendar you use while traveling to note down expenses *less than $75* for which you don't have receipts.

Also keep in mind that the church can reimburse you for all church-related expenses, including the travel items listed, as a tax-free fringe benefit.

Income
Here is a checklist of income items to help you keep track:

Church salary $ _____
Taxable fringe benefits $ _____
Honorariums $ _____
Baby-sitting $ _____
Odd jobs $ _____
Sideline business $ _____

The following are some more expenses to help make sure you don't forget any. You can use these expenses if they are church related, or if you or your wife (see Proverbs 31) has a sideline business:

Expenses
Please list every possible expense you can think of—every time you write down an expense, your tax bill goes down.

Accounting fees $ _____
Advertising and promotion $ _____
Appraisal costs $ _____
Auto and truck expenses $ _____
Bad debts $ _____
Bank service charges $ _____
Business-club expenses $ _____
Business gifts $ _____
Business license
   and regulatory fees $ _____
Business services $ _____
Business taxes $ _____
Carry forwards of losses
   from past years $ _____

Cleaning and care of business areas $ _____

Commissions $ _____

Consulting fees $ _____

Contract labor paid $ _____

Convention expenses $ _____

Depletion $ _____

Discounts allowed customers $ _____

Dues and publications $ _____

Donations $ _____

Educational expense to maintain
  or improve present skills $ _____

Employee benefits and programs $ _____

Employee medical expenses $ _____

Equipment rental $ _____

FICA and unemployment tax
  paid for employees who work
  for you $ _____

Freight/shipping $ _____

Insurance $ _____

Interest: mortgage $ _____

Interest: finance charges, etc. $ _____

Janitorial service $ _____

Keogh plan contributions $ _____

Laundry and cleaning $ _____

Legal and professional fees $ _____

Library expenses $ _____

Meals and entertainment $ _____

Moving costs $ _____

Obsolescence of
  business assets $ _____

Office expense $ _____

Organizational expenses $ _____

Pension and profit-sharing plans
  and contributions $ _____

Personal property tax $ _____

Postage $ _____

Professional journals $ _____

Purchases during the year $ _____

Real estate tax $ _____

Rent on business property $ _____

Repairs $ _____

Safe deposit box $ _____

Sales returns, refunds,
  rebates or allowances $ _____

Sales tax $ _____

Security and guard services $ _____

Service or maintenance
  contracts $ _____

Start-up expenses $ _____
Stationery $ _____
Storage fees $ _____
Supplies and materials $ _____
Telephone $ _____
Theft and casualty losses $ _____
Tools $ _____
Trash collection $ _____
Travel $ _____
Uniforms $ _____
Utilities $ _____
Wages paid to children $ _____
Wages paid to employees $ _____
Wages paid to spouse $ _____
Miscellaneous

_____ $ _____
_____ $ _____
_____ $ _____
_____ $ _____
_____ $ _____

Did you have an office in your home for this business?

❏ yes   ❏ no

If yes, you'll need the information in this section:

Total square feet in your home   _____
Square feet used for your business   _____
Date you purchased your home   _____
How much did you pay for
   your home? $_____
Cost of any improvements you
   have made to your home $ _____
Rent $ _____
Interest $ _____
Taxes $ _____
Insurance $ _____
Utilities $ _____
Repairs made to your home for
   personal use $ _____
Repairs made exclusively for your
   business $ _____

Appendix 5
One of the Best Tax Shelters for Ministers

The Minister's Housing Allowance— Best Tax Break in America

The minister's housing allowance, found in Section 107 of the Internal Revenue Code, is probably the most valuable, and least understood, of all tax breaks open to ministers.

Many pastors do not get the full advantage of this important tax benefit.

The housing allowance is not a recent tax benefit.

How far back does the housing allowance go?

This tax benefit goes back in its present form for more than 40 years, and in one form or another for more than 70 years. It is nearly as old as the income tax law itself. To me, this is a confirmation that "governments are ordained of God," and that God has seen to it that the U.S. Tax Code contains generous provisions for ministers.

The housing allowance as it exists today was written into the Internal Revenue Code of 1954, 45 years ago.

Before that, a parsonage allowance was enacted as Section 22 of the Internal Revenue Code of 1939.

Even before that, a minister could exclude the value of a parsonage under Section 213 of the Internal Revenue Code of 1921, which was 78 years ago.

This benefit didn't "just come out." It has been around almost as long as there have been income tax laws in this country (these started in 1913).

Incidentally, the Congressman who introduced Section 107, which is the present-day housing allowance, said the reason for it was to help ministers fight the godless world system because ministers generally made less money than other people, and needed an extra tax break. Who says the Lord doesn't ordain governments?

Who Qualifies?

To get a housing allowance, you have to be an ordained minister and perform one of the following:

1. Duties as a minister, in a church or elsewhere, as long as you are under the authority of a church;
2. Teaching duties in a religious school run by a church;
3. Various duties by an ordained minister, such as associate pastor, evangelist, missionary, music director, educational director or school principal, and administrator of a religious organization such as a missions board or a church.

There are some other possibilities, but these are the main ones that apply to local churches.

Just keep in mind that whatever the duties may be, they must be performed under the authority of a church, for church purposes and you must be a "minister" for tax purposes, under the five-part test (described later in this appendix, and also in appendix 3, under the section "Who Qualifies for Special Tax Treatment as a Minister").

First, we're going to talk about what the housing allowance is; then we're going to look at the items you can spend the housing allowance on; and then we'll talk about the limits on how much you can take. After that, we'll finish up by seeing some more advanced ways to use the housing allowance to benefit you as a minister.

The original purpose of the housing allowance was to give a minister a way to build up retirement equity because many ministers do not have other sources of retirement income.

It has always puzzled me why this particular means was chosen, because the only way a minister could get any income out of a house was to sell it. My guess is the thinking is that if a minister owns a house outright, and doesn't have a house payment, then the only expenses he or she will have are food, utilities and personal incidentals. Thus, retirement income will not be absorbed by rent or a mortgage payment.

In any event, the housing allowance does provide a way for a minister to have an asset that is worth something at retirement, which effectively reduces your outgo, and can also provide a sizable amount of cash, even if you have to move to get at it.

Essentially, the housing allowance means that you, as a minister, can have your church pay for your house tax free, even though you own the home personally.

In some cases, as we'll see, you don't even have to report the housing allowance on your income tax return. (Although ministers who are not exempt from Social Security tax have to report their housing allowances on Schedule SE.)

The church can pay the housing allowance to you and you can pay for your housing expenses, or the church can pay your housing expenses directly. It doesn't matter which one.

However, whichever method you choose, be sure to keep *good records* of what has been paid and by whom, and *keep receipts for everything*. The rule is: *If you can't prove it, you lose it.*

One of the limits on the housing allowance is the amount you actually spend on housing-related items, so you must be able to show by written proof the amounts spent.

Another thing that does matter is that the housing allowance must be designated in advance in your church minute book.

You might be wondering: *What about last year, when we didn't write down my housing allowance.* Well, fortunately for you, the law doesn't say that you have to designate the housing allowance *in writing*, (but it does have to be *in advance*). However, the easiest way to prove you designated the allowance in advance is to have it written down.

Here's what to do: If you can remember the approximate date you and the board met and talked about the amount of your housing allowance, make minutes of the meeting, date them as of the date the meeting was held and have each director or trustee (directors and trustees are the same thing in a nonprofit organization) sign the minutes. This is called "memorializing" a meeting. It is *not* backdating. Backdating is where something happened in July, but you date it back in January. Memorializing is where something happened in January, but wasn't recorded and written down until July. Memorializing is perfectly legal; just be sure to have everyone present at the meeting sign the minutes as witnesses.

Ideally, this should be done at the first of the year (or even December of the preceding year). The housing allowance designation should be recorded in the official church minutes.

I would recommend that you follow this method in the future, even if you haven't done so in the past.

If your past church practice did not include written church minutes designating your housing allowance, other written evidences that can be acceptable are the following:

- A designation that is part of a written employment contract;
- A line item in your church budget that shows the amount of your housing allowance;
- A written designation on the check you received for your housing.

In one known case, the IRS allowed an oral designation. However, *don't rely on this case*; it is only for use when all else fails. There is reason to believe that this case might not work in many church situations. The best advice always is: *have it in writing.*

Just be sure you designate a *specific amount* (this should be a dollar amount) for *each minister* on staff. Avoid generally designating a blanket housing allowance for all staff ministers. Mention the minister's name and the exact dollar amount of that minister's housing allowance.

Another thing you should do when you designate each minister's housing allowance is to state that the allowance is "for 1999 and every year thereafter until changed by the board of directors."

That way, if the allowance is accidentally overlooked next year, there will be a "safety net" to cover it.

Of course, it is better to designate the housing allowance specifically for each staff minister each year, but having a "safety net" can prevent the accidental loss of the housing allowance, for example, when staff changes cause items to be overlooked.

What happens if you designate the housing allowance in January, and in July you discover that you didn't designate enough? A little known fact is that you can *redesignate* the housing allowance anytime during the year, and the new amount will be effective for the rest of the year following the redesignation.

What happens to amounts spent *before* the increased designation? They are probably lost because the requirement is for designation *in advance* of actual payment.

This means the housing allowance is *not* a reimbursement kind of expense. It is an *advance payment* kind of expense.

So designate much more than you think you actually will spend on housing. This cannot ever hurt you; it can only help. *Under*designation causes the tax benefit to be lost forever, while *over*designation makes sure that nothing is lost.

Here's why that is important: You get a housing allowance for the *least of*:

- The amount designated by your church;
- The amount you spend;
- The amount your home would rent for, furnished, plus utilities.

Because you can control the amount designated, it should *always be more* than either of the other two amounts so that nothing is lost because the designation was too low.

Incidentally, there's no limit on how much housing you can designate. *That's right, you can designate 100 percent of your salary as housing if you like.*

Just remember the other two limits still apply. If you spend less than 100 percent, the limit is what you spend. Or if you own your home, and the Fair Rental Value is less than what you spend, the limit is the Fair Rental Value rule.

Where 100 percent designation of housing usually can come in handy is for teachers in Christian schools.

Often, nearly all their salary is spent on housing because often their spouse works as well. It may be a tremendous benefit to them to have 100 percent of their salary designated as a housing allowance.

Although the IRS has told me it would not raise the issue of husband/wife allocation in this kind of situation, I still have the following recommendation for Christian-school teachers whose spouses work a secular job:

- What might happen is the IRS could say yes, the housing allowance was designated all right, but it was the money from the secular job that paid the housing.
- If you have a joint account, how could you prove any different?
- So if you're a Christian-school teacher receiving a housing allowance, and your spouse works a secular job, why not open a *separate checking account* for your housing check?
- Then use that account to pay *all housing expenses* previously listed.
- That way, you have proof that your housing allowance was used to pay actual housing expenses.

Again, the IRS has told me it wouldn't raise this issue, but I say better safe than sorry.

What Can You Include in the Housing Allowance?

The purpose of the housing allowance is to *provide a home for the minister*. That's what the law says, and that's about all it says. The following is exactly what it says:

Section 107, Internal Revenue Code:

In the case of a minister of the gospel, gross income does not include—

(1) the rental value of a home furnished to him as part of his compensation; or

(2) the rental allowance paid to him as part of his compensation, to the extent used by him to rent or provide a home.

(1) the rental value of a home furnished as a part of compensation *[this means a church-owned parsonage]*; or

(2) the rental allowance paid as part of compensation, to the extent used to rent or provide a home *[this means the cash paid to you by the church for your housing allowance, as long as you spend it on qualified housing items]*.

You may already know about the basics, such as:

- Mortgage principal;
- Mortgage interest;
- Real estate taxes;
- Insurance (on home and/or contents for fire, theft and liability);
- Rent;
- Utilities—electric, gas, water, sewer, trash, cable TV, telephone, firewood.

You might have heard about some of the lesser-known items, such as:

Down payment. Your church can pay for the down payment on your house, and it will be tax free to you. But, if the down payment is more than about 5 percent of the purchase price of the home, one of the limitations we'll talk about in a few minutes (the Fair Rental Value limitation) may come into play. As we'll see later, it is best to spread the down payment over more than one year to get the full benefit of the housing allowance.

Real estate commissions, attorney fees, escrow fees, points, organization fees, etc. *related to purchasing a home.*

Furniture and furnishings. All your furniture and furnishings can be paid for with the housing allowance.

Appliances. The housing allowance can be used to buy your refrigerator, stove, dishwasher, washer/dryer, vacuum cleaner, lawn mower, television, food processor, mixer, electric can opener, carpet and rug-cleaning equipment, etc.

Repairs to appliances, furniture and furnishings. Any time you have to fix appliances or repair or re-cover furniture or other furnishings, these expenses can be paid for out of the housing allowance.

Special assessments for streets, sewers, sidewalks, etc.

Often Overlooked Items That Can Be Included

Here are some other items that many ministers don't realize can be included in the housing allowance. Some of these items were subjects of actual court cases allowing a minister to have that item in his or her housing allowance:

- Pest control;
- Plumbing services;
- Kitchen items, plates, silverware, dishes, utensils, cups, glasses, cookware, etc.;
- Household cleaning supplies, detergent, wax, polish, tissue, mops, brooms, light bulbs, trash bags and so forth;
- Carpet, curtains, rugs, drapes, linens, towels, pictures, paintings, frames, decorator items, paint, wallpaper, door keys, locks and so on;

- Insurance on furnishings;
- Maintenance;
- Landscaping, lawn services, gardening, shrubbery, sod, grass seed, fertilizer, fencing;
- Improvements such as adding on rooms or other structural changes;
- Repairs to the home itself, and other upkeep.

If you are adding on rooms or making other major home improvements, you probably should consider obtaining a home equity loan to cover these so you can spread out the payments over more than one year. (See the section on home equity loans.)

New floors, new carpets and new cabinets have been allowed as part of the housing allowance. Almost any kind of remodeling can be included in the housing allowance.

About the only things you *can't include* in the housing allowance are (1) food, (2) maid services and (3) personal toiletry items (such as soap, shampoo, toothpaste and personal paper products).

You can keep track of housing items by having a separate receipt for food and one for housing items when you go to the store. Then put your housing receipt in a special folder marked "HOUSING" where you keep all your housing-related receipts. At the end of the year, it becomes a simple matter to total your actual housing expenses. This also serves as written proof of these items for tax purposes because you must always be able to prove your actual housing costs.

Home Office

So what happens if you have a home office and you also receive a housing allowance?

As of the date of this 2000 edition of *ClergyTax®*, you basically cannot have your cake and eat it, too.

In other words, to the extent you receive nontaxable income, that is, the housing allowance, you cannot also take a deduction for your home office.

What you have to do is *prorate* your home office expenses (and actually other minister's business expenses as well) based on the percentage of your income that is made up of "nontaxable income," in other words, your housing allowance.

Now, would you like that in English? Okay, let's say you receive $10,000 in salary and $10,000 in housing allowance.

You have $2,000 in home office expenses.

Because half of your total compensation as a minister is housing allowance, half of your home office expenses cannot be deducted.

One-half of $2,000 is $1,000. That leaves another $1,000 that can be deducted. (The IRS could also take the position that because *all* housing expenses are covered by the housing allowance, *none* of your home office expenses can be deducted. You might argue against this position if your housing allowance were underdesignated and you had excess housing expenses not paid for by your housing allowance.)

You can apply the same basic rule to your other minister's business deductions. This is called the *Deason Rule*. It's based on a tax case where the judge said the minister had to do that.

Of course, not all ministers follow the *Deason Rule*. But the IRS does follow it, and if your return is audited, that is the position they will be taking.

If the *Deason Rule* expenses we're talking about are *not* housing related, then of course you could argue that because housing by definition can only cover housing allowance items, *Deason* cannot possibly apply to other minister's business expenses because it is impossible for a minister to spend any exempt housing allowance on such items.

That raises one other little question: Can you even take a home office deduction these days if you are a minister?

Most likely not. Because, in the case of a minister, the one requirement that will be hard to meet is that the deduction applies only if you cannot have an office at the church: In other words, the home office must be your only office.

Very few ministers ever meet this requirement.

However, there will be some who do. Many ministers starting an independent work have the church office in their home, and that is the only church office. They may very well qualify for the home office deduction.

Maybe the minister has decided to work out of his home exclusively, and he only comes to the church to preach on Sundays, and perhaps for counseling appointments, which are held in counseling rooms. But otherwise, he has no office space at the church. It is possible that this situation will qualify for the home office deduction.

If you have a borderline situation, better check with your tax advisor about how to handle it.

Otherwise, most ministers won't be able to take a home office deduction anyway.

Considering the advent of a recent case, the IRS can now possibly take the position that even if your home office is your only office, preaching at the church might be considered where you actually earn your money, and if so, they might disallow the home office deduction.

Bottom line: Probably the best argument for a home office deduction for a minister is when starting a new church, and the only office space is actually in the home. At press time, we could find no cases fitting this particular situation.

Lastly, as a footnote, some commentators have suggested that a minister could commute from the home office to the church for purposes of turning what would normally be commuting mileage into business mileage, even if no home office deduction were available.

There is some logic in this position because a home office is still an office whether or not it is deductible for tax purposes.

When you drive from one business location to another (that is, home office to church), that becomes business mileage. Commuting, on the other hand, is considered driving from home to work.

One thing is certain, whether that idea will work or not, the IRS won't like it.

To increase your chances on this one, keep the same kind of home office records you would need to substantiate a deduction for a home office.

Keep a detailed mileage log in your car.

Ministers who would benefit most if this kind of arrangement were allowed would be those who live a great distance from the church, say 30 miles or more each way. They might save up to $1,000 in taxes each year if their commuting mileage were considered business mileage instead.

Again, this is what is known as an *aggressive tax position*, so consult your tax advisor to increase your chances of winning.

New home office rules: Due to a new tax law, a minister now qualifies for a home office deduction if: (1) the office is used by the minister to conduct administrative or management activities of a church or ministry, and (2) there is no other fixed location where the minister conducts substantial administrative or management activities of the church or ministry. As under present law, deductions will be allowed for a home office meeting the above two-part test only if the office is exclusively used on a regular basis for church or ministry business by the minister and, in the case of a minister who is an employee, only if such exclusive use is for the convenience of the church. This new rule applies beginning January 1, 1999.

How Do You Determine What Your Housing Allowance Should Be?

It's fairly simple, really.

It all depends on whether you (1) rent your home, (2) own your home or (3) live in a church-owned parsonage.

If You Rent Your Home

Just take your monthly rent and add your utilities and the other items previously listed that you spend to keep up your home. That's your monthly housing allowance.

To illustrate:

Your rent is $500. Your utilities are $150. Your monthly housing allowance is $500 + $150, or $650 a month.

Can you take anything else on your housing if you rent?

Good question. Nobody really knows, but I'll tell you what I think.

The IRS regulations allow for rental of a home, furnished. You either have to rent the furniture or buy it. So I believe that all the allowable items can be included when you rent your home.

Here's a rule of thumb I use (it's not found in any official IRS code or publication; it's only one man's wild guess of what will probably fly): Take your rent, multiply by two, add your utilities, and as long as you don't spend more than this amount on total housing expenses of every kind, you're probably all right.

For example, if your rent is $500, multiply by two and you get $1,000, add utilities of $150, and you have $1,150 a month, or $13,800 a year. That probably represents the upper limit of what you can spend each year, if you rent, on all housing items combined.

Just don't get carried away, for example, with water slides, tennis courts and oversize swimming pools, if you know what I mean.

Remember also that no one knows for sure exactly what the correct number really is for renters. Often the agent will try to decide on a case-by-case basis. However, if you stay in the range I mentioned, you're certainly better off than if you're way above that range. Some commentators believe that a minister who rents a home can take all his or her actual expenses, no matter what they are (within reason). I personally tend to agree with this position, and I have never seen it challenged in an actual audit. This position also lines up exactly with what the Code says. However, because the precise rules here have never been clarified to my satisfaction, I would say there is still some doubt in this area, and each individual minister is going to have to take the position that feels comfortable.

Know that because there really isn't any guidance on the subject from the government, they can provide guidance at any time, which may or may not agree with what I'm telling you right now.

Shame on them if they don't agree.

If You Own Your Home

You start with what your home is worth. That is, what would your home sell for if you sold it today?

Then take 1 percent of that amount (just divide the value of your home by 100). You will then have about what your housing allowance should be each month.

You can add utilities to that, and you can probably add at least another 50 percent of the monthly amount (just divide the monthly amount by two) for furniture rental.

Let's look at an example:

Let's say your house is worth $100,000. Divide that by 100. That means you have a housing allowance of $1,000 a month. Add your utilities, say $200, and then 50 percent of the monthly amount for furniture (that's $1,000 divided by two), or $500. So your total housing allowance would be $1,000 + $200 utilities + $500 furniture, or $1,700 a month.

You might be wondering, *where is that rule written down?* Answer: *It isn't.*

Here's what we're trying to do: We're trying to find the Fair Rental Value of your home, furnished, plus utilities. That's what you can have for a housing allowance if you own your home.

When you take 1 percent of the value of your home, that should be approximately what it would rent for unfurnished. You might have to adjust that up or down depending on the area of the country in which you live and your neighborhood. But 1 percent of the value is probably a good place to start when trying to find an idea of what your home would rent for. If you want a more exact figure, just look in the paper and see what homes are renting for where you live. Or check with a realtor.

When we take 50 percent of the monthly number, we are trying to figure out what it would cost to rent your furniture. The figure 50 percent is just approximate. If you want an exact number, go to a store that rents furniture, and see what it would cost you to rent all the furniture you have in your house. (I guarantee you will be surprised how much it will be.)

Then you add utilities, whatever they happen to be.

Area of Country	Value of Home	Monthly Housing Allowance
Northeast	$125,000	$1,875
Southeast	$ 75,000	$1,125
Midwest	$100,000	$1,500
Plains	$100,000	$1,500
Southwest	$100,000	$1,500
West Coast	$200,000	$3,000

These figures are kind of "bare minimums," and are approximate, based on what I've seen around the country for ministers pastoring independent churches that have 200 or fewer members. If your church is larger, you may have to adjust these figures. If your church is just starting out, they may have to be adjusted downward. (Remember that utilities are not included in these numbers, so don't forget to add them.)

Please keep in mind, these are just my own ideas, because no official numbers anywhere give this kind of information.

Ministers are always asking me what is "safe," and I would think these numbers are as close as you could come for an estimate.

So far, I haven't seen the IRS challenge a minister in the given area who lived in the value of home indicated. That doesn't mean they won't. But friends, you all know it would be hard to find a livable home for less, wouldn't it?

(As I said, the previous numbers are all "plus utilities." That means you have to add the cost of utilities to the number given for "Monthly Housing Allowance," which, incidentally, is just an estimate. Your housing allowance has to be considered reasonable. In case you haven't noticed, America is not exactly gung ho on ministers making scads and scads of money. If that statement sounds odd to you—maybe you've been living on the mission field.)

In practice, it is unlikely the IRS would ever disallow a housing allowance equal to your mortgage payment, plus the cost of renting the furniture in your house, plus utilities, (as long as the entire allowance is spent on home-related items, and as long as the cost of your home falls within the realm of "reasonable compensation" for services rendered at your church).

Can you use the housing allowance that is in excess of your mortgage payment for other home-related items? Yes. Here again, only if the total housing allowance paid is Fair Rental Value or less.

To illustrate, let's say your housing allowance is $1,400 a month. Your home would rent for about $800 a month, and your furniture would rent for $400 a month (that's $1,200 a month total). Your utilities are $200 a month. But your actual mortgage payment is only $600 a month.

So you take your housing payment of $1,400 for the month of July, and spend it as follows:

Mortgage payment—$600

Utilities—$200

That leaves you $600.

It's time to buy a new couch, and they're having a sale at Furniture City on the latest sofa for exactly $600.

That's an allowed item for your housing allowance, so you can buy it and use up the rest of your housing payment for July.

But let's say August comes around, you again have $600 left over, and nothing to spend it on. Can you still exclude that $600 from your income and not pay tax on it?

Not unless you spend it on an allowable housing item or items before the end of the year. Why not?

Because back in 1984 Jimmy Swaggart owned his home free and clear. But he still received $500 a month in housing allowance. The IRS told him he had to pay income tax on the $500 a month. He took it to court—but the judge sided with the IRS.

Now all ministers have to pay tax on any housing allowance they do not actually spend on allowable housing allowance items.

If You Live in a Church-Owned Parsonage

The value of the parsonage, if you had to pay rent on it, is your housing allowance. This is automatic, and doesn't even have to be stipulated in the minutes.

If you live in a church-owned parsonage, of course the church can remodel it, add new rooms (or a garage or pool), supply cleaning supplies and so forth, and none of this would be taxable to you.

Your utilities, and any other items previously listed, can be part of your housing allowance if the church designates them in writing and pays you a parsonage allowance. You just have to be able to document that you spent all the parsonage allowance on these items. Any part of the allowance that was not spent on parsonage-related items has to be included in your gross income for income tax purposes.

In other words, let's say you live in a church-owned parsonage. The church pays your utilities and has already put furniture in the home before you move in.

Then they give you $500 extra a month, and put this part in the minutes, and call it a "parsonage allowance."

In September, here's how you spend the money:

$200—new end table

$100—year's supply of floor cleaner and light bulbs

$100—lawn care

$50—put on a new backdoor screen

$25—buy a gallon of house paint to do some touch-up work on the garage door

$25—take your family to the movies for the first time in 10 years to see *Swiss Family Robinson*

How much of the $500 is nontaxable and can be excluded from your income for income tax purposes? (Remember, *all* housing allowance is taxable for *Social Security tax* purposes, *unless* you are exempt from Social Security tax because you have filed Form 4361 and have been approved.)

Answer: $475

Only the part you spent on the movies does not qualify as an allowable housing allowance item, and thus it must be included in your regular salary for income tax purposes.

(As a footnote, Congress wanted to give equal treatment to ministers who own their own homes. So the same things a church could provide for a parsonage you can include in your housing allowance if you own your own home. That's the reason for this rule.)

Unless you are exempt, you have to pay Social Security tax on the Fair Rental Value of the parsonage in which you live. Probably the minimum value this can be is 5 percent of the appraised value of the parsonage. For example, if the parsonage is worth $100,000, the lowest the annual Fair Rental Value can be is $5,000.

Again, this is purely an estimate. (Factors such as church use of the parsonage, number of ministers occupying the parsonage, no choice in matter of parsonage assigned, etc., can also lower the rental value, sometimes dramatically.)

In the previous example, for Social Security tax purposes, a minister who pays Social Security tax would have to include the Fair Rental Value, the utilities and the $475 spent on housing items. None of this would be included for income tax purposes. The $25 spent on the movies would be included for *both* income and Social Security taxes.

A minister who is exempt from Social Security tax only has to include the $25 in his income tax. The rest is completely nontaxable.

All right, for all you eagle-eyed tax experts out there, ministers really don't pay *Social Security tax* per se. It's actually *self-employment tax*. Big deal. Everybody calls it Social Security tax because that's what it is. Self-employment tax is merely Social Security tax for people who are self-employed. Because the tax code treats *all* ministers as self-employed for Social Security tax purposes (even if they are considered employees for income tax purposes), ministers always pay self-employment tax (unless they are exempt) instead of Social Security tax. See how simple and obvious? See why I just call it Social Security tax and forget it?

Interest and Taxes

Don't forget that not only can your housing allowance pay the interest and taxes on a home you own, but then you can also turn around and deduct the same interest and taxes *against your other income!*

It sounds almost too good to be true. But after all, the Lord has ordained governments, and in this case, the U.S. tax laws provide a tax shelter to ministers that is truly exciting.

Here's an example:

Your salary is $26,500 a year. This is your total compensation.

Your mortgage payment is $500 a month (yes, those were the good old days; remember, this is just an example).

Your real estate taxes are $500 a year (don't you wish).

So you are paying $6,000 in mortgage payments a year, and $500 in taxes, for $6,500 total.

The church designates from your salary a housing allowance for you of $6,500 a year (of course, you would want a larger housing allowance after you read this section of *ClergyTax*® to cover all the other items that can be included).

This $6,500 you receive is *free of income tax.* (You still have to pay Social Security tax on it unless you have elected out of Social Security tax by filing Form 4361.)

So the church reports $20,000 as your salary on your W-2. You report the same amount on your tax return as your income.

Now, let's assume that of the $6,000 you paid to the bank in mortgage payments, $5,500 of that is interest (shocking isn't it? but that's exactly what happens in the early years of a mortgage loan).

Then, on Schedule A, you can *deduct* the $5,500 in interest, *and* the $500 in real estate taxes.

Guess what? That leaves you only $14,000 of income! (The $20,000 you reported as income, less $5,500 interest and less $500 taxes.)

Do you see what is happening?

The same money you received as *cash* in the form of a housing allowance can now be deducted against your other income!

It's quite amazing—and also quite legal.

This one idea can be worth *thousands of dollars* a year in tax savings. Over the life of a typical mortgage, it could be worth literally *tens of thousands of dollars!*

Many ministers sadly are not taking advantage of this perfectly legal *tax shelter* written into the law just for them.

Be sure your accountant knows the ins and outs of this one—the potential savings are enormous.

As long as a regular mortgage is used to buy or build a home, the interest is deductible up to $1 million. Interest on a home equity loan up to $100,000 is also deductible on Schedule A of your tax return. (Check the following information for whether home equity interest is allowable as part of your housing allowance.)

If you did *not* take a deduction for mortgage interest and taxes on your home because you thought receiving a housing allowance meant you couldn't take these deductions, you can still amend your return for 1997, 1998 or 1999 and claim these deductions. You do this by filing Form 1040-X, amended income tax return. (You may also still be able to amend your 1996 return, depending on when it was filed—see your tax consultant.)

Home Equity Loans—How They Can Still Be Used for Tax-Free Housing Savings to Some Extent

Here is how a minister used to be able to get a great tax benefit:

Let's say your home is paid off, so you can't really take advantage of the housing allowance. Because remember, if the money isn't actually spent on housing, it doesn't qualify as a minister's housing allowance, even if it meets all the other tests.

So if your home is paid off, you don't have a mortgage payment, and you lose the amount that would otherwise have qualified as the payment on your house.

Let's say, using this particular idea, you go down to your friendly bank (is there such a thing?) and borrow, for example, $20,000 against your paid-off home.

You tell the bank you will put the whole $20,000 in a savings account or CD (Certificate of Deposit), provided they charge you 1 percent more on the loan than they pay you on the savings account or CD. They never have to actually give you the money, so often many banks will agree to this because it is "found money" to them.

Then let's say the loan has to be paid off in five years. That would be about $425 a month in payments. So your church designates a housing allowance of $425 a month to pay on your housing loan.

The $425 a month is not taxable to you (except for Social Security tax purposes, as we mentioned earlier). At the end of five years, when the loan is paid off, the $20,000 in the CD is all tax free to you. It is sitting there in the bank, tax free, as a retirement account, or whatever.

You only pay tax each year on the interest the bank pays you on the CD.

Pretty neat, huh?

There's only one catch: The IRS came along and issued a private-letter ruling disallowing this great idea.

This tells you that they will not go along with it.

What if you have already taken out the loan and set up everything?

You are probably safe for tax years *before* 1991, the year the ruling came out, because usually the IRS won't disallow a tax break *retroactively* if there wasn't any guidance on it before. (The IRS doesn't usually go back more than three years during an audit.)

These years are now closed and can't be audited anyway.

Of course, they don't have to be this lenient. Even if they aren't, they can only go back three years. So you would only owe income tax for the last three years on the payments you made on the home equity loan. You still keep the deduction for the interest on the loan. It's just that you are not getting the exclusion for the housing allowance on the amount of the payments.

However, if instead of putting the loan money in a savings account you used it to buy, add on to or substantially improve your home, you may have a loophole.

The ruling didn't address what would happen in this case. I think the IRS would have a tough time disallowing payments on a home equity loan as part of your housing allowance where you actually used the loan proceeds on allowable housing allowance items.

So if you can use loan proceeds to add real value to your home, the housing allowance in effect can be used in this kind of situation to build equity in your home that otherwise would not be there.

A private-letter ruling doesn't carry too much weight in the world of tax law; it just tells you what the IRS thinks about a particular subject.

Private-letter rulings are changed and overturned all the time, and they only apply to the particular person the letter ruling was written to.

So the jury is still out in this area. I'll be reporting further developments in upcoming editions of *ClergyTax*®.

Another possible way to build extra equity in your home tax free is to make additional principal payments when you make your mortgage payments. So far, this strategy has not been disallowed by the IRS. However, no ruling specifically approves it either.

Spreading Out the Down Payment on Your Home

It is also a good idea to spread out the down payment on a home because you probably cannot cover even a 10 percent down payment with the housing allowance for one year (because, when added to your other housing expenses, it would be more than the Fair Rental Value we discussed).

The easiest way to do this is with a loan, preferably from a bank. However, your church can also legally lend you the money.

That is, *legally* from a federal standpoint. In other words, it's okay with the IRS (although not particularly recommended).

However, some states do *not* allow churches to lend money to their pastors (or anyone else who is a director; some of these states may offer a loophole if the pastor is not on the board of directors).

So check with your attorney about state law in your particular state before trying this.

If the church lends you the money, I recommend the following safeguards in addition:

1. Put everything in writing.
2. Charge yourself the market interest rate .
3. Actually record the church's second mortgage down at the courthouse.
4. Make regular monthly payments on the church's loan.

Of course, the church can pay you additional housing to cover the loan payments, and designate these as housing. This is how you spread out the down payment and keep it tax free as part of your housing allowance (which is still subject to Social Security tax, though, unless you are exempt).

Home Equity Loan to Buy a Car

Here's one of those ideas that tax-wise ministers use to cut their taxes:

You can use this idea if for one reason or other you choose to own your own car instead of having the church provide one for you. (See appendix 3 of this book for how to set up a church auto plan for a minister.) Some possible reasons for this might be that you may be thinking of taking another pastorate and want to take your present car with you, or perhaps one of your cars is used by your wife solely for personal use.

You probably know that personal interest is no longer deductible on your income tax return, and this includes interest on a car loan.

You probably also know that interest on a home equity loan *is* still deductible (although if the loan proceeds are used to buy a car, the loan payments probably do not qualify for housing allowance treatment).

So just put these two principles together: Take out a home equity loan and *pay off* your car loan.

You still *owe* the same amount of money. However, there is one big difference: Before, you might have had, say, $2,000 or $3,000 of interest that was *nondeductible*.

But now, you have a *$2,000 or $3,000 income tax deduction!*

If you are in the 15 percent tax bracket, this could save you $300 to $450 a year in taxes!

If you are in the 28 percent bracket, you might save $500 to $800 each and every year!

It's so very simple: just a little paperwork, and then writing a payoff check on your car loan.

Added benefit: The interest on a home equity loan is often lower than on a straight auto loan—even from the same bank.

Land Contracts for Parsonages

Let's say you live in a church-owned parsonage, but you want to own your own home.

You might consider *buying the parsonage*. But you (or your board) may be wondering, *is this legal?*

Absolutely, as long as you follow a few simple rules.

Important rule: All transactions in which a minister buys something from the church must be done in such a way that the church receives *full value* for what is sold.

In other words, *no discounts* on the price of the parsonage. Have a Realtor appraise the parsonage, and then pay *full price*.

Otherwise, if the church were right now to outright *give* you the home, say, by just handing you a warranty deed, then you would have to include the *full value* of the home, less the allowable housing allowance exclusion, on your W-2 for this year. Not a fun thought, because if the home is worth $120,000, and if allowable housing were $20,000, you might owe about $33,000 in extra income tax. Believe it or not, ministers have actually made this little mistake before.

What about the down payment?

Often, homes are sold using what is known as a *land contract*. This kind of agreement helps when the buyer does not want to put down a lot of money for one reason or another.

Here's How It Works

The buyer puts down $1,000 or $2,000 to cement the deal. The seller prepares a warranty deed, but does *not* give it to the buyer (at least not just yet).

The deed goes into escrow, which just means that someone trustworthy holds the deed for both parties until a later date.

Having the deed in escrow protects the seller in case the buyer doesn't pay.

The buyer is also protected, because the seller has already signed the deed in the buyer's favor.

The buyer then makes payments according to the land contract for a certain number of years.

The entire price of the home may be paid according to the contract, or after a few years the buyer may refinance the contract at a bank and pay off the seller at that time.

When either (1) the home is paid for under the contract, or (2) the contract is paid off by a bank loan, then the deed is given to the buyer by the escrow officer.

Are you ready for a really *amazing idea*?

You can have the church pay you a housing allowance, and then use the housing allowance to pay off the land contract, month by month!

I know several pastors who are using this simple idea to build retirement equity in a home—tax free. So far, the IRS has been allowing these kinds of arrangements, as long as they are done at a fair market value.

Another way to accomplish this is to have the church buy a lot, build the home you want and then sell it to you by land contract. Just be sure the board of directors agrees on this arrangement. Usually, it has been my experience that the board wants to help the pastor have a good home, and this is an excellent (and painless) way to do it.

Caveat: As of the date of publication of this edition of *ClergyTax*™, this wonderful idea has not yet been torpedoed by the IRS. However, as with all wonderful tax ideas, there is always a chance that the IRS—or more likely Congress—will take away a perfectly fabulous tax-saving loophole. We'll let you know in future editions of *ClergyTax*™ if this ever happens.

One other thing you need to watch out for with land contracts: In some states (such as Texas) that usually exempt parsonages owned by a church from property taxes, it is possible that the county or state may take the position that as the land contract is paid off, the minister will owe property taxes in the same proportion as the ownership interest that is being built up. Say, for example, that a land contract is half paid off. The tax assessor might say that the minister owes half the property tax on the house now. This can happen even when the deed is still in the church's name. Consult a local attorney who is skilled in real estate matters to draft language that will help solve this potential problem.

New Pastors and New Churches

If you have just started a new church, and you as the pastor still have a secular job, here's an idea for you:

Use the earnings from your secular job to make contributions to the church. Then the church will have enough funds so that it can pay you a housing allowance, which is, of course, free of income tax.

I have seen the IRS accept, without audit, tax returns of ministers who gave up to 30 percent of their income to their church.

The law says you can legally give up to 50 percent of your (adjusted gross) income to your church.

Be prepared to show that there was no obligation on the part of the church to pay you a housing allowance in return for your donations.

You are allowed to give up to half of your adjusted gross income in any year to your church (any excess can also be carried forward for five more years). And the church is allowed to designate a housing allowance for you.

Because this idea may seem too good to be true, again, as I just mentioned, the IRS or Congress can always take away a perfectly good loophole anytime they want to. We'll keep you posted in *ClergyTax*® each year whether there have been any cases or changes in this area.

Cleaning

Your accountant may have told you that you can't include housecleaning in your housing allowance. This is a subject of some debate, but the accountant is probably right.

The regulations for Section 107 say the only two things you *can't* include in the minister's housing allowance are (1) food, and (2) servants.

Does housecleaning come under the heading of "servants"? Some people think so, and others think not.

Among the people who think so are the IRS. But there may be a way to accomplish the result, *legally*.

Let's say you have some church functions in your home.

You might put some language in your church minutes, such as the following:

> RESOLVED, that the pastor uses the parsonage for Bible studies, church leadership meetings, counseling appointments, housing for guest speakers and other church activities. The board wishes to reimburse the pastor for the expense of cleaning and maintaining the home due to these activities. The amount of such expenses up to $150 per month is hereby designated to be reimbursed to the pastor each month for expenses incurred in cleaning and maintaining the parsonage in good order suitable for church activities.

See how easy it is?

Just remember, this is one idea that has had no court cases yet, so while it probably works under what we know of current law, a judge or the IRS or Congress could change it any time.

I would class this idea as one for adventurous pastors only. But I also think it at least gives you some possible grounds for taking a cleaning allowance as a reimbursement, rather than as part of your housing allowance.

Record Keeping

Why is it that many pastors are notoriously poor record keepers?

I am sure it could have nothing to do with the fact that they work 18 hours a day. And someone said the call of God shorts out the business-related chip. (Or maybe God doesn't call too many people who have the business chip.) Whatever.

Anyway, many pastors I know personally don't like record keeping, and avoid it whenever possible.

So here are some ideas to make it as painless as possible.

Incidentally, record keeping is *essential*. It is *not* an option. It is the way you can laugh at an audit because you know your records are in order.

Here Are Some Thoughts

1. *Have your secretary do it.* Just be sure she has the sort of vinegarlike personality that goes along with a well-organized, record-keeping kind of person. If your secretary is happy, friendly, great with people, *don't* let her do your record keeping for you. You'll be sorry. But if she's a little caustic, somewhat domineering, counts paper clips and rubber bands, and can't understand why everyone else drives so slow, *she's the one.*

2. *Have your wife do it.* Some pastors think their wives shouldn't take care of the business. But sometimes their wives are much better at it than they are. Make this a matter of prayer.

3. *Have an accounting service do it.* For example, many accounting firms provide an accounting service that does church financial statements each month for $150. For an extra $65 or so, they take care of all the pastor's record keeping as well. You may have such a service where you live. The money is well spent when you receive complete statements each month so that your records are in good order and everything you need for tax time is right there at your fingertips creating no additional work on your part.

4. *Do it yourself.* If you are one of those rare pastors who has the "business chip," and you can find an extra hour or two a week to devote to record keeping, you can always do it yourself.

One or Two Other Ideas

Create one folder you use *only* for housing-related expenses.

Every time you pay a bill or buy something related to your home, just throw it in that folder. Then, at the end of the year, backing up your housing allowance with hard-copy receipts will be a snap.

When your wife goes shopping, have her get one cash register tape for food, and another cash register tape for everything else.

Then put the second tape in your housing folder. This way you won't miss all those smaller items that can really add up during the course of a year.

Social Security Tax Considerations (Schedule C)

I have news for you: As a pastor, you may very well be in the *50 percent income tax bracket.* Sound incredible? Well see for yourself:

Regular income tax starts in the 15 percent bracket. If your taxable income is more than about $41,000, then the bracket jumps to 28 percent. Social Security tax is another 15.3 percent. If you're in the 28 percent income tax bracket, that brings you up to 43.3 percent. Does your state have an income tax or a sales tax? Yes? Then, welcome to the 50 percent tax bracket, pastor!

It is unfortunate, but *Social Security tax is payable on your housing allowance.*

This is true even though the housing allowance is *exempt from income tax.*

Does this sound confusing? Basically, there are now *two income taxes.*

One is the *regular income tax,* which is what you get from the Tax Table each year in the back of your 1040 instruction booklet.

The other one is the *Social Security tax,* which is supposed to be saved up for your retirement, but actually it is being used to pay *current bills of the government. None of this money is being saved.*

There is nothing in the Social Security system but a bunch of Treasury bonds that can't even be traded on the open market.

It's basically just IOUs from the government to itself.

So the Social Security tax amounts to *a second income tax.*

Fun, huh?

Anyway, if you are still in the Social Security system, you have to put the amount of the housing allowance on Schedule SE to your tax return, and pay 15 percent tax on it. (Actually, it's 15.3 percent.)

Is there any way around this? One way, possibly.

(I know my good friend Rich Hammar is going to hate this section, so Rich, please just close your eyes until you get to the next section.)

Let's say you're paying Social Security tax, and it's too late for you to elect out. (See the section later in this appendix for a new case that may allow some ministers a "second chance" to elect out of Social Security.)

You receive all the salary and all the housing—but let's say your wife has been working close to full-time and not being paid.

Nothing is wrong with changing things to reflect economic reality.

In other words, you can *pay your wife the same salary you would have to pay to replace her.* You can also reduce your own salary if the church can't afford to pay her otherwise.

This change just reflects the reality of what has been happening all along.

If your wife legitimately works in the ministry, and she qualifies to be ordained, your church can ordain her.

If your wife objects on scriptural grounds to *receiving* benefits from the government for her work in the ministry, then she may elect out of Social Security by filing Form 4361.

One commonly cited Scripture for electing out of Social Security is: "Those who preach the gospel should receive their living from the gospel" (1 Cor. 9:14)—*not from government handouts.*

(It is interesting, incidentally, that if a minister has at least 40 quarters of nonministerial work paid into Social Security when Form 4361 is filed, the retirement benefit *remains vested.* How's that for consistency by the government?)

Then the church could designate your wife's pay as housing (up to allowable limits). The result is that your wife's salary does not have to be reported for Social Security tax purposes, and no tax is due for Social Security tax.

You still have to pay Social Security tax on your own compensation, but the situation is much improved.

Now I want to let you know that I have checked this strategy at least *four times* directly with the IRS. I actually talked to people in the Exempt Organizations Division in four separate areas of the country (including the national office), and they all agreed that this idea would work.

I even asked them why a loophole big enough to drive a truck through was allowed to exist. They said that so few people were in this kind of situation (one spouse paying Social Security tax and the other not), that they just didn't bother about it.

But of course, they could start bothering about it any time they want to.

My advice: Only set this up if you understand that I merely have an oral okay from the IRS on it. Guess what that's worth?

You're right: an oral okay from the IRS and 50 cents will still get you a cup of coffee (unless you go to Starbucks).

Also know that this whole idea could be torpedoed *any time* by Congress or the IRS.

Lastly, do not try this on your own. Get a competent attorney or CPA to set it up for you.

Then keep praying that nothing changes. Put any tax savings in your retirement plan so that if the Lord tarries, you'll have something on which to retire.

Retired Ministers

A church may officially designate up to 100 percent of the pension paid to a retired ordained minister as a rental allowance. (The IRS will allow designations of 100 percent of salary or pension, as long as the other limits on the housing allowance are observed. Remember, they are the lesser of (1) how much you actually spend on housing items, and (2) the Fair Rental Value of your home.)

Here Are the Rules:

1. A part (or all) of a retired minister's pension is designated as a housing allowance by the trustees of the church pension fund.
2. The retired minister no longer works for the local church, and relies on the pension for (part or all of) his or her compensation.
3. The pension is compensation for the retired minister's past services to a local church(es) or denomination.

Pension payments to a retired minister that are designated as housing allowance are now exempt from Social Security tax by law. Utilities are also covered. This benefit is retroactive, and retired ministers who paid Social Security tax on their housing allowances in 1995, 1996 or 1997 can file amended returns to claim a refund.

If I were you, I would be sure to make arrangements for retirement housing way before you are ready to retire.

You want to get the approval of the church board of directors, as well as the new pastor who will be taking over the church.

You want everything in writing, spelled out, legally correct.

Things tend to run smoother this way.

Don't wait until you have left your church, and then as an afterthought, call the new pastor and ask if he or she would mind paying for your housing now.

See what I mean?

If you are nearing retirement age, this is an important tax benefit that should not be overlooked in your retirement planning.

Teachers in Christian Schools

A little-known fact is that many church-school teachers can be ordained and receive a minister's housing allowance.

This is often quite legal when your church operates a Christian school, no matter what grade levels are offered.

Even where all subjects taught at a church school are not taught with emphasis on religious principles and religious living, most Christian schools operated by churches are considered to be integral agencies of the church that operates them.

(Be careful if your school is separately incorporated from your church—you need to consult a lawyer.)

This means that a church can designate a housing allowance for ministers who teach or have other duties in the school run by the church.

Most ordained ministers serving in a church school as head of a department, or as a teacher or administrator (or someone who has overall management duties) will be eligible for a housing allowance (and their compensation rules will be the same as any other minister).

As long as the teacher or other school staff meets the five-part test of a minister for tax purposes (described later in this appendix, and also appendix 3), they automatically qualify for a housing allowance designation, if the school is owned and operated by the church.

One essential part of the five-part test is being ordained, so you must ordain any teacher to whom you plan to pay a housing allowance.

You should also inform any newly ordained teachers who begin receiving a housing allowance that they have the option of electing out of Social Security, as far as their church-related wages go.

One last item: The situation is somewhat less clear if the church is operating a day-care center.

The reason for this is that a day-care center is not normally considered a school for tax purposes.

Many of the housing allowance cases talk about schools, colleges and universities where ministers teach or have other duties.

Whether a day-care teacher or administrator would qualify to be ordained and receive a housing allowance is an open question.

You should consult your tax advisor before setting up this kind of arrangement in a day-care situation.

Traveling Evangelists and Guest Speakers

To designate a housing allowance for a traveling evangelist:

1. Give the evangelist his offering check.
2. Along with the check, give him a statement signed by an officer of the church.
3. In the statement, state that the offering was designated in advance as a housing allowance for the evangelist.
4. The evangelist will not have to pay tax on the amount he uses to provide his home (subject to the Fair Rental Value rules), as long as it is a permanent home (not a travel trailer—although a clever CPA might find a loophole even there).

While we're at it, any amount paid to a guest minister that is designated as housing allowance does not have to be reported on a 1099 at the end of the year.

Guest speaker housing is subtracted from the total offering for 1099 purposes.

Examples:
Total guest offering is $700, and the whole amount is designated as housing. No 1099 is required because housing is not reportable on either a 1099 or a W-2 in any case.

Total guest minister offering is $1,000, and $500 is designated as housing. No 1099 is necessary because the non-housing part of the offering is $500, and this is less than the $600 threshold required before a 1099 has to be issued.

The Fine Print

Who is a minister? Here are the tests:

1. Ordained, commissioned or licensed;
2. Conducts religious worship;
3. Administers the sacraments;
4. Performs management functions in your church;
5. Considered to be a spiritual leader in the church.

You have to have number one, and any two of the other four, to qualify as a minister for tax purposes. If you are ordained by a local church, be sure your articles or bylaws allow your church to ordain ministers.

Some recent cases seem to say that you must have all five items to qualify as a minister for tax purposes. Other cases say you only need three (number one and any two others).

Personally, I think the better view is that at least three out of five will qualify you as a minister for tax purposes, as long as you are ordained.

Qualified Tax Breaks

As a minister, for what tax breaks are you qualified?

1. The housing allowance;
2. Exemption from Social Security tax (but you have to file Form 4361, sometimes as soon as 16 months from your ordination, to qualify; don't wait to file on this important benefit if you decide to opt out of the Social Security system);
3. Exemption from withholding on both income and Social Security taxes (see appendix 1).

These benefits are only available in regard to your earnings *as a minister*. They do not apply to secular earnings, even if you are ordained and considered to be a minister for tax purposes.

These important tax breaks are discussed in detail elsewhere in this book.

Be sure to study still other tax breaks that are available to you as *the employee of a corporation—such as a health plan or church auto.*

Reporting Requirements

The housing allowance is *not reported* by your church on either your W-2 or 1099, whichever you receive.

The housing allowance, incredible as it may seem, is *not reported* by your church at all, anywhere. The church only reports your net salary, not including any part of your housing allowance.

The housing allowance only shows up on your tax return in *one place*: Schedule SE.

Schedule SE is where you pay your Social Security tax (actually, for ministers it's called "self-employment" tax, but most people just call it Social Security tax anyway because that's what it is).

Because the housing allowance is subject to Social Security tax, you report your housing on Schedule SE and pay Social Security tax on it.

(Don't forget to deduct your unreimbursed church-related expenses on Schedule SE also. This should be done pursuant to IRS Publication 517. These expenses are usually the same ones you can also deduct on Schedule A or Form 2106—see a tax professional for advice about specific items.)

If you are exempt from Social Security tax (because you filed Form 4361 and received an approved copy), then you don't have to file Schedule SE at all (unless you have secular earnings not subject to FICA withholding), and so your housing allowance will not appear anywhere on your tax return.

Now, what happens when you receive $20,000 in housing, but you only spend $18,000 in actual housing expenses that you can prove?

You simply put $2,000 on line 21 of your 1040, and label it "excess housing allowance." That's all there is to it.

Here's one other way to handle any housing allowance excess, if you're "Johnny-on-the-spot" in getting your tax information together in early January:

If you know how much your housing allowance excess is before the end of January (for example, because you added up all your housing receipts and subtracted the total from the amount paid to you as a housing allowance), you can tell your church treasurer, and the excess can just be added to your W-2 or 1099. This eliminates the need to put the excess on line 21 of your 1040.

...

Equity Allowances for Ministers Who Live in Parsonages

Because ministers who live in parsonages build up no equity in their homes, many churches pay them so-called "equity allowances" so they will be able to buy a home when they retire, or at least have the money on which to live.

The IRS has ruled that these equity allowances *cannot* be excluded as parsonage allowances in the year they are paid.

This means that to avoid tax on an equity allowance, it must be put into a tax-exempt church retirement plan each year. A "403(b) Plan" is such a retirement plan.

The money builds up tax free, and is available to the minister on retirement to buy a home, or for any other purpose, and is taxable when the money is taken out at retirement. (Withdrawals properly designated as housing may reduce the tax burden.)

If you live in a church-owned parsonage, my advice is to ask your board for an equity allowance.

It's only fair after all because the church is getting the equity in the parsonage you otherwise would have had available for retirement.

In my personal opinion, it's almost always better for you to own your own house rather than reside in a church-owned parsonage.

For example, besides the equity issue, you can't write off the interest on a mortgage loan on your parsonage, while you *can* do so if you own the home.

The church can't write off the interest on a parsonage loan either because the church is tax exempt and has no need for deductions.

So a terrific tax benefit may be completely wasted if you live in a church-owned parsonage.

That's also true of the deduction for real estate taxes: The tax benefit is completely lost in the parsonage situation (at least in states that don't grant property tax exemptions for church-owned parsonages).

If living in a church-owned parsonage is unavoidable for some reason, at least be sure the minister receives an equity allowance to compensate him or her for the loss of equity buildup.

I would go one step further and recommend an additional amount to compensate for the tax benefit that is lost. In other words, have the church pay the tax the minister would have avoided if he or she could have deducted the interest and any real estate taxes on the parsonage.

The amount of tax thus paid by the church should be included as salary on the minister's W-2 at the end of the year (unless it is paid to the minister's qualified retirement plan as an additional contribution).

To Sum Up

All the housing allowance items previously listed are available in the following situations:

1. If you live in a church-owned parsonage, the Fair Rental Value is automatically excluded from income (but must be included on Schedule SE for Social Security tax purposes).
2. If you live in a church-owned parsonage, the items listed above can be excluded from income, if the church designates the payment of a *parsonage allowance* in advance, and you actually spend the money on these items. (Even though excluded from income, these items are still taxable for Social Security purposes unless you are exempt.)
3. If you rent a home, the items listed above can be excluded from income, if the church designates the payment of a *rental allowance* in advance, and you actually spend the money on these items. (Even though excluded from income, these items are still taxable for Social Security purposes unless you are exempt.)
4. If you own your home, the items listed above can be excluded from income, if the church designates the payment of a *housing allowance* in advance, and you actually spend the money

on these items *and* the amount of the housing allowance does not exceed what the home would rent for furnished (you can add utilities to this amount). (Even though excluded from income, these items are still taxable for Social Security purposes unless you are exempt.)

Appendix 6
Sample Minutes for:
Church Health Plan

Then, upon motion duly made, seconded, and unanimously carried, it was

> RESOLVED, that the following be and it hereby is adopted as and for the (1) official health plan and (2) the official health expense reimbursement policy of the church:

1. The church may pay the health insurance premiums of full-time ordained, commissioned or licensed ministers and their dependents, as well as other staff, who are considered employees of the church for tax purposes, and even though ordained ministers may be considered self-employed for Social Security tax purposes.

2.a. The church may reimburse all out-of-pocket health expense costs of full-time ordained, commissioned or licensed ministers and their dependents, as well as other staff, who are considered employees of the church for tax purposes, and even though ordained ministers may be considered self-employed for Social Security tax purposes.

2.b. In the event that any health expense is not paid for by health insurance, if any, paid or provided by the church or other payer or provider, the church may pay directly or may reimburse any church minister or other staff for any such noncovered expense that is paid by the minister or other staff person. The intent of this policy is to pay deductibles, any other forms of coinsurance that are not paid for by health insurance, if any, paid or provided by the church or other payer or provider, and in general, all "out-of-pocket health expense costs" incurred by a minister or other staff member of the church. The term "out-of-pocket health expense costs" shall include, but not be limited to, (1) deductibles not covered by health insurance, or (2) any other amounts not covered by any health insurance paid or provided by the church or other payer or provider, or (3) any other amount not covered by health insurance, whether or not the minister or other staff member is currently covered by health insurance, or was so covered at the time expenses were incurred, for all physicians, medicine, hospital costs and all other costs commonly thought of as medical costs, including, but not limited to:

    insurance premiums
    prescriptions
    dentists
    lab fees
    medical supplies
    humidifier
    Medicare premiums
    doctors
    hospitals
    nursing costs
    air conditioning, electricity, hotel, transportation and like costs where directed by physician or allowed by law, special equipment (such as eyeglasses, dentures, hearing aids, special shoes, etc.)
    other costs allowed by statute, regulation, case law or other authority

2.c. This health expense reimbursement policy covers all health expenses that would otherwise be deductible on

Schedule A of the Form 1040 income tax return of the minister or staff member who receives the reimbursement, and the minister or staff member must provide the church with the same type of proof as would be needed to claim a deduction on such Schedule A, in order to receive a reimbursement or direct payment from the church under this policy. Ministers may receive reimbursement under this policy by presenting receipts to the church treasurer in compliance with the official general reimbursement policy of the church.

2.d. In the event the IRS shall find that the health expense reimbursement policy of the church is taxable to a staff minister(s) because it discriminates in favor of highly paid or control employees, then the church shall include such taxable payments on the W-2(s) issued to such minister(s) as a taxable fringe benefit.

Appendix 7
Sample Minutes for:
Accountable Reimbursement Policy

The directors then discussed that recently several tax law changes have been made in the rules for reimbursement of church expenses to church ministers and staff. The directors felt that the church has been in compliance with these new rules, but that it would be well to write this policy in the church minutes, in addition to and in clarification of any other entries that may already exist in the minutes.

The directors discussed the fact that the Code now requires certain procedures to ensure that reimbursements to church ministers and staff members are not income to them. The church has been following these procedures during the past years of 1998 and 1999, and the directors wish to have the procedures written down, along with any other minutes that exist. The directors want to make it clear that the church intends all reimbursements paid by it to qualify as reimbursements paid according to an adequate accounting to an employer under an accountable reimbursement plan, so that they do not have to be reported as income by ministers and church staff receiving the reimbursements.

Then upon motion duly made, seconded and unanimously carried, it was

> RESOLVED, that the following be and it is hereby adopted as and for the official reimbursement policy of the church until amended or rescinded:

1. The church may reimburse church ministers and staff for expenses incurred on church business, for items purchased for church use, for all ordinary and necessary expenses required for the exercise of their ministry and work within and on behalf of the church, and for the carrying out of other nonprofit religious purposes of the church. However, only expenses properly substantiated according to this policy will be reimbursed.

2. Expenses that are considered by the church to be ordinary and necessary for the performance of ministry include, but are not limited to, the following: (1) On-the-job transportation; out-of-town travel to church conferences, assemblies and continuing education; where auto expenses are involved, the staff member may elect reimbursement for actual expenses, or at the standard mileage rate currently allowed by the IRS: for 1999 this rate is 31 cents per mile; (2) other professional continuing education by correspondence and locally; (3) professional materials (books, magazines, journals, papers, tapes, films, videos, office supplies, etc.); (4) business meals, business entertainment and business gifts for conducting church business and developing pastoral relationships; (5) expenses for meals, cleaning and supplies in connection with church functions held at a minister's home or parsonage, including expenses connected with the housing of guest evangelists to save hotel costs; (6) professional dues and fees for memberships in religious and civic organizations; (7) business telephone; (8) professional equipment (communion, office, library, audio-visual, music, etc.); (9) the purchase and cleaning of clergy vestments used in church worship services; (10) child and dependent care expenses, when incurred to enable both minister and spouse to attend church functions for which the presence of the spouse is important to the continuing ministry of the church; when provided gratis by an on-premise church day-care facility; or when equal to or less than the lesser of $5,000 per year, earned income, or spousal earned income.

     The church, at its discretion, may elect to pay any expenses under this policy by direct billing upon receiving receipts and vouchers from the minister.

The church recognizes the professional nature of ministry and recognizes the right of the minister to use professional judgment when incurring expenses. The church has the right to limit the amount of ministry expense reimbursements on the basis of reasonableness in amount. A minister or staff member may deduct the amount of any unreimbursed expense(s) as allowed by law.

3.   To receive reimbursement, a church minister or staff member must account to the church treasurer by filing expense reports for reimbursable expenses no less often than monthly, and in no event more than 60 days after any particular expense is incurred. These reports shall provide "adequate accounting" to the church, as that term is used in the Code, which means that they must provide the same kind of proof as would be necessary to substantiate a deduction taken for the same expenses on the minister or staff member's own income tax return.

Accounting for expenses to be reimbursed must be made with substantiating records, receipts and/or contemporaneous personal statements of expense such as an account book or diary, showing date, amount, place, business purpose and business relationship. These receipts, and/or statements, shall be of the same nature as would be required to substantiate a deduction on Form 2106 under Schedule A of Form 1040 Federal Income Tax Return, Schedule C of Form 1040 or otherwise pursuant to currently published IRS tax regulations or publications. This policy shall be deemed to include whatever IRS regulations or other requirements are announced under new Internal Revenue Code Section 4958 after the date of these minutes.

4.   Reimbursement shall be made only for the amount actually incurred. In no event shall a reimbursement be for an amount greater than the actual expense incurred. In the event that reimbursement shall inadvertently be made for any amount greater than expenses accounted for, the person receiving such overpayment shall promptly return it to the church within 90 days of the date the associated expense was incurred, or within 30 days of the overpayment, whichever is sooner.

5.   The church minister or staff member receiving a reimbursement under this policy shall maintain adequate receipts and records covering the reimbursement for at least four years from the date of the reimbursement, and shall provide copies of the same to the church treasurer upon request.

6.   No expense reimbursed according to this accountable reimbursement policy shall be reported as income on any Form W-2 or Form 1099 wage statement issued to any minister or church staff member receiving such reimbursement(s).

7.   In the event any question arises about the amount of any expense to be reimbursed in any instance, the decision of the church treasurer shall be final.

Appendix 8
Fringe Benefits for Ministers

Fringe Benefit	Available to Minister on W-2?	Available to Minister on 1099?	Free of Income Tax?	Free of Social Security Tax?	Can Church Discriminate in Favor of Minister?
Housing Allowance	Yes	Yes	Yes	No	Yes
Church Auto	Yes	No	Yes	Yes	Yes
Church Retirement Plan—403(b)	Yes	Yes**	Yes	Yes	Yes
Group Term Life Insurance—$50,000	Yes	No	Yes	Yes	No
Other Life Insurance	Yes	Yes	No	No	Yes
Health Insurance Premiums Paid	Yes	No	Yes	Yes	Yes
Out-of-Pocket Health Expenses Paid	Yes	No	Yes	Yes	Yes*
Self-Funded Medical Reimbursement Plan	Yes	No	Yes	Yes	Yes*
Disability Insurance	Yes	No	Yes	Yes	Yes
Income Tax Paid by Church for the Pastor	Yes	Yes	No	No	Yes
Social Security Tax Paid by Church for Pastor	Yes	Yes	No	No	Yes
Business Expenses Paid by Church	Yes	No	Yes	Yes	Yes
"Cafeteria" Fringe Benefit Plans	Yes	No*	Yes	Yes	No
Child Care	Yes	Yes	Yes	Yes	No
Qualified Tuition Reductions	Yes	Yes*	Yes	Yes	No
Educational Assistance —$5,250***	Yes	Yes	Yes	Yes	No
Educational Reimbursement —$Unlimited	Yes	No*	Yes	Yes	Yes
Moving Expense Reimbursement	Yes	Yes	Yes	Yes	Yes
Travel—Personal	Yes	Yes	No	No	Yes
Travel on Church Business	Yes	Yes	Yes	Yes	Yes
Telephone Calls, Copies, Snacks, Parking	Yes	Yes*	Yes	Yes	Yes
Church Bookstore Discounts	Yes	No*	Yes	Yes	No
Meals and Lodging for Convenience of Church	Yes	Yes*	Yes	No	Yes
Meals in Church-Run Cafeteria	Yes	No*	Yes	Yes	No

* Indicates no reliable IRS guidance at present for these items.
** New law change.
*** This benefit expires after May 31, 2000. (Benefits for graduate level courses expired June 30, 1996.) Note: Legislation is currently pending that would apply the exclusion for church-provided education assistance, for both graduate and undergraduate education, to courses beginning on or before June 30, 2004. The above table represents the best information about ministers' fringe benefits available at the present time. We plan to update this information as needed. Consult your tax advisor for questions about specific items. **Please Note:** Under the new "intermediate sanctions" law, all fringe benefits paid to a minister should be noted in the church minutes. The IRS has said it is considering an exception that would allow some nontaxable fringe benefits to be paid that were not written down in the minutes, but at press time, this exception had been proposed, but not finalized. So it is still a good idea at this point to make sure that all fringe benefits, taxable and nontaxable, are carefully noted in the minutes prior to being paid to any minister or on his or her behalf.

Appendix 9
Intermediate Sanctions, Overview

A new scheme of penalty taxes has been passed unanimously by Congress, and will apply to churches, pastors and church board members. The Senate even passed the law by unanimous consent, without voting, because of broad bipartisan support. President Clinton signed the bill into law on July 30, 1996. This new federal legislation will dramatically change how ministerial compensation is determined.

The law contains tax penalties on ministers and their family members who receive "excess benefits" in a business relationship with a church or religious organization and on exempt organization board members who participate in such relationships knowing the excess benefits existed.

For many years, Section 501(c)(3) has required that no part of the net earnings of a church inure to the benefit of any private individual, as a basic condition for tax exempt status.

The new law is technically known as new IRS Code Section 4958, which imposes penalty taxes (i.e., "intermediate sanctions") where ministers and their family members, and church board members, participate in what is called an "excess benefit transaction." Both the minister (the "insider"), the minister's family members and any director having foreknowledge of the excessive nature of the transaction can be subject to the new tax. For the first time, this penalty tax falls on the individual, and not the church.

The law contains many new provisions that will affect church administration and the compensation provided for ministers. The law provides for the following:

1. If a minister receives an "excess benefit transaction," then the IRS will levy a 25 percent penalty tax on the amount of compensation that exceeds reasonable compensation (i.e., the amount that ordinarily would be paid for like services by like enterprises under similar circumstances). The new law, Code Section 4958, defines an "excess benefit transaction" as *any transaction in which an economic benefit is provided by an applicable tax-exempt organization directly or indirectly to or for the use of any disqualified person if the value of the economic benefit provided exceeds the value of the consideration (including the performance of services) received for providing such benefit. For purposes of the preceding sentence, an economic benefit shall not be treated as consideration for the performance of services unless such organization clearly indicated its intent to so treat such benefit.* The focus here is on "excessive" salary payments. Unless a given salary and/or benefit is clearly documented in church minutes, it can automatically be subject to the new penalty taxes. The following situations can be considered "Excess Benefit Transactions" under the new law:

    a. A minister is a party to a non-Fair Market Value transaction with the church. Non-Fair Market Value transactions might include the purchase of a minister's home or car by the church for a price in excess of Fair Market Value; the receipt by a minister of personal items, such as office furniture or equipment, from the church at a reduced rate; or the church cosigning on loans and assuming risk that is more than its equity in the asset. The new law identifies "market value" as the benchmark for determining the penalty tax and not the cost of the benefit to the church. This means that even if the cost to the church is little or nothing, the IRS will still use the Fair Market Value of the benefit when figuring penalty taxes. For example, if a church or ministry has its own plane, the new law may treat travel of a spouse (even if the cost to the church is minimal) as an "excess benefit transaction."

    b. A minister receives unreasonable compensation from the church. Unreasonable Compensation Transactions might include the payment of excessive compensation to a minister for his or her services; excessive compensation to a member of senior church management; and excessive bonuses to any "insiders," including ministers or senior church management under an incentive compensation arrangement.

 c. A minister receives salary payments based on the income of the church in a way that violates the private inurement rules. Revenue Sharing Transactions can include incentive compensation arrangements when bonuses, salary or other compensation paid by a church is an uncapped percentage of its gross or net revenues; it can also include "revenue stream" transactions, which are arrangements in which a ministry pledges its future gross or net revenue stream to a seller of goods, someone providing services to the church, or an "insider."

2. If the IRS can adequately prove that church board members knew the minister received an "excess benefit," then church board members will be jointly and severally liable for a 10 percent penalty tax on the "excess benefit." The maximum penalty per church board member is $10,000.

3. If the minister and/or church board members do not render corrective action on a timely basis (i.e., 90 days from the mailing date of the notice of deficiency for the first penalty tax [the 25 percent or 10 percent penalty tax]), then an additional 200 percent penalty tax will be levied against the "excess benefit." Ministers can be subject to this additional penalty tax. Corrective action is defined under the law as *undoing the excess benefit to the extent possible, and taking any additional measures necessary to place the organization in a financial position not worse than that in which it would be if the disqualified person were dealing under the highest fiduciary standards.* In other words, a minister who received unreasonable compensation must pay back to the church any excess compensation received from the church in order to correct the violation.

Churches will have to satisfy the following "safe harbor" requirements (referred to as the "rebuttable presumption of reasonableness") established by Congress to avoid these penalty taxes:

1. Ministerial compensation and corresponding fringe benefits must be approved by a board of directors or trustees (or a committee thereof) that was composed entirely of individuals unrelated to and not subject to the control of the insider (i.e., the minister) whose compensation is being set (a reciprocal approval arrangement, in which an individual approves the insider's compensation and the insider, in turn, approves the individual's compensation, is also prohibited).

2. The church board must obtain and rely upon appropriate data as to comparability (e.g., compensation levels paid by similarly situated organizations, both taxable and tax-exempt, for functionally comparable positions; the location of the organization, including the availability of similar specialties in the geographic area; independent compensation surveys by nationally recognized independent firms; or actual written offers from similar organizations competing for the insider); and

3. The church board adequately documented, in detailed minutes, the basis for its determination (e.g., the record includes an evaluation of the individual whose compensation was being established and the basis for determining that the individual's compensation was reasonable in light of that evaluation and data).

Similar safe harbor requirements exist for property sold, purchased or otherwise transferred between a church and an insider. The transaction must be approved by an independent board using appropriately comparable data and the board adequately documented its determination of the reasonableness of the transaction. If the safe harbor rules are followed, intermediate sanction penalty taxes can be imposed only if the IRS develops "sufficient contrary evidence" to rebut the probative value of the evidence developed by the parties to the transaction. This is not very likely, given the staffing and budget problems at the IRS. A church board of directors (or committee thereof), acting according to normal fiduciary duties of care and loyalty, will in most cases protect the minister against the penalty tax. For example, if a minister purchases a home or other property from a church, suitable documentation (i.e., a professional appraisal) of the reasonableness of the transaction must exist.

The new law includes the following provisions:

- If the safe harbor rules are satisfied, the burden of proof for determining excessive compensation will be on the IRS.
- All payments of personal expenses and fringe benefits must be documented *ahead of time* in the minutes of the church board meetings. Failure to comply, and to report such expenses and fringe benefits correctly on the W-2, can preclude these items from the protection of the safe harbor. All salary and fringe benefits must be approved *in advance of payment* and documented in church board meeting minutes.
- The "excess benefits" penalty taxes apply to the minister, disqualified persons and the board members individually, not to the church or evangelistic association.
- Minister's family members (which includes the minister's spouse, their children, grandchildren, great-grandchildren, brothers and sisters, and the respective spouses of all these family members) must be listed as "disqualified persons" on the organization's Form 990. These individuals are prohibited from receiving "excess benefits." In addition, they must not participate in decisions associated with determining their individual compensation packages. Evangelistic associations who fail to file their 990s in a complete and timely fashion can now be fined up to $50,000 *per return*. Increased Form 990 disclosure requirements are already incorporated into new versions of the form. Even more changes are expected on the 1999 form.
- Evangelistic associations will be required to notify the IRS of changes in their governing board, changes in their Certified Public Accountants and/or any payments (by related parties) of $100,000 of more to "control employees."
- The new law will require evangelistic associations to make available at least three years of financial information to anyone that requests such information. Failure to comply can result in a $5,000 penalty per request. However, the Treasury Department is expected to allow a partial waiver of this new disclosure rule if an organization can prove it is the target of an organized harassment campaign. Consequently, implementation of this penalty is suspended until 60 days after these new Treasury rules have been published.
- Under the new law, evangelistic organizations are required to report any penalty taxes paid by disqualified persons for excess benefit transactions on the subsequent filing of Form 990.
- The new law defines a "disqualified person" as an individual who is in a position to exercise substantial influence over the affairs of a tax-exempt organization. This includes church officers, directors or business managers. "Disqualified persons" also include a minister's family members. The law indicates that any person who was a disqualified person at any time during the previous five (5) years retains this status.
- Under the new Act, an administrative title (e.g., officer, director and/or trustee) does not automatically render an individual a disqualified person. In addition, a House Committee Report indicates that substantial influence may be exercised even by a nonemployee, such as a large donor, and thus satisfy the definition of a disqualified person.
- The new law covers compensation packages developed on or after **September 14, 1995**—1997, 1998 and 1999 compensation packages must be reviewed immediately for compliance under safe harbor requirements. The new law does not apply to excess benefits arising from a transaction under a written contract that was already signed on September 13, 1995, and which remains in force at all times thereafter, and no material terms of the contract have changed. For compensation packages that were set up after September 13, 1995, and before January 1, 1997, the safe harbor can be invoked if the rules are satisfied within 90 days after the compensation is approved.
- Effective **January 1, 1997**, safe harbor is *only available* if the requirements have been satisfied prior to the payment of any benefits.

- The organization may pay liability insurance premiums to protect the minister and the board against the new penalty taxes. However, this benefit must be included (and documented) in the compensation package.
- Churches are allowed to use a compensation consultant's opinion (which can include figures from secular organizations) for determining compensation.
- In most cases, the IRS will use the new penalty tax *instead of* revoking the church's exempt status. But the IRS will still be able to assess the new penalty taxes, *and* revoke an organization's tax-exempt status. The House Committee Report explains that Congress intends that the new penalty taxes will be the only action taken by the IRS, unless "the tax-exempt organization no longer operates as a charitable organization." The new law makes no changes in the private inurement prohibition, or the IRS's ability to revoke exempt status.
- The normal three-year tax statute of limitations applies.
- If a minister or board member is assessed the new penalty tax, but can prove reasonable cause and the absence of willful neglect, and timely corrective action relative to the transaction has been taken, the penalties can be abated. ("Timely" means within 90 days from the mailing date of the notice of deficiency for the first penalty tax—that is, either the 25 percent or 10 percent penalty tax.) To undo the excess benefit, the exempt organization must be repaid, or made whole to the extent possible. The exempt organization should be placed in the same position as it would have been had there been no excess benefit. However, it appears that a minister would only be required to undo the transaction to the extent possible and to make restitution. This might be quite important where a hardship existed, or where an asset purchased from the exempt organization had been resold.
- If the church believes it is paying the minister a nontaxable benefit, but later the IRS says it is taxable, then the church can pay the tax the minister owes.
- The new law may permit churches to compensate a minister based on an increase in the income of the church, for example, because the minister helped the church to grow.
- The personal liability penalty for church payroll taxes has been removed for church board members who serve in a volunteer, unpaid capacity, who do not participate in the daily financial activities of the organization and have no actual knowledge of the failure to collect and pay the taxes.

Important Questions for Ministers to Consider

Q. Who is covered by the new law, and is thus subject to the 25 percent penalty tax on excess benefits?

A. *Anyone* (including a minister's family members) who can exercise substantial influence over the organization, and this need not even be an employee or a director. The key element is the amount of control the individual has over the financial affairs of the organization. Intermediate sanction provisions impose excise taxes on section 501(c)(3) public charity (not private foundation) and section 501(c)(4) organization "disqualified persons" and organization managers who engage in excess benefit transactions. These transactions could take the form of unreasonable compensation for services or non-Fair Market Value transactions for goods or other property.

Q. Who is a disqualified person?

A. The term "disqualified person" is now defined as anyone in a position to exercise substantial influence over an organization. The term "disqualified person" includes the individual's spouse, brother or sister (and their respective spouses), child, grandchild or ancestor (and their respective spouses) of a person who exercises substantial influence. Also covered are corporations that are controlled at least 35 percent by a disqualified person, or a corporation that gives 35 percent or more of its benefits to a disqualified person.

Q. Will the new law change the treatment of payments to volunteers?

A. It is possible that churches will now have to treat benefits to volunteers as compensation. However, a contrary argument can be made in cases where the services rendered greatly exceed the benefits received.

Q.   What happens if the penalty tax is imposed on a minister?

A.   If penalized, a minister must:

1.   Restore (pay back) the benefit to the organization;
2.   Pay the penalty tax;
3.   Pay interest on the penalty tax;
4.   The church may also be liable for withholding tax penalties;
5.   Board members may also be liable for penalties.

Q.   To what compensation does the new law apply?

A.   To any compensation paid on or after September 14, 1995 (the law is retroactive).

Q.   To what benefits does the new law apply?

A.   The law applies to the following types of benefits (this list is not inclusive of all benefit types):

1.   Contributions to pension and profit-sharing plans;
2.   Deferred compensation plans;
3.   Low- or no-interest loans;
4.   Life, liability and other insurance provided;
5.   Personal use of a church auto;
6.   Airplane, boat and train fares;
7.   Personal use of club memberships;
8.   Personal expenses (housing allowance, food and entertainment, furniture, legal/tax advice, etc.);
9.   Other housing expenses, such as home remodeling and maid service;
10. Travel and entertainment expense reimbursements under nonaccountable plans;
11. Tuition and related education fees and expenses;
12. Vacations;
13. Limousines;
14. Health spas;
15. Theater/sports tickets and related expenses;
16. Buying something from the church for less than Fair Market Value;
17. Selling something to the church for more than Fair Market Value;
18. Loans to the church at a high rate of interest;
19. Leases or other contracts from the church that are favorable to the disqualified person.

Q.   What can be done to protect the minister and the church against the new law?

A.   Take the following steps:

1.   Establish a precise conflict of interest policy that ensures that all compensation and other related business decisions are made in such a way that objective standards are followed, and that insiders are not influencing the decisions on their own behalf. The IRS recommends the following:
     a.   Require disclosure by interested parties of financial interests and all material facts relating thereto.
     b.   Have procedures for determining whether the financial interest of the interested person may result in a conflict of interest.
     c.   Have procedures for addressing an identified conflict of interest.
     d.   Have procedures for adequate record keeping.
     e.   Ensure that the policy is distributed to all trustees, officers and members of committees with board-delegated powers, including requiring an annual statement from such persons.

    f.   Have specific procedures for applying the policy to a compensation committee.

2. Structure compensation within the safe harbor parameters.

    a.   Completely document a determination of reasonableness of compensation by unrelated individuals (e.g., an independent board, Certified Public Accountant or attorney).

    b.   Determine whether compensation and benefits are comparable to those paid by other organizations (use a compensation consultant or reputable study).

    c.   Clearly document the basis for determining compensation and corresponding benefits (taxable and nontaxable).

    d.   Documentation must be contemporaneous, that is, it must be written down before the compensation is paid.

    e.   Any benefits that are excluded can be subject to the new penalty taxes.

    f.   Document the conclusion that the compensation and fringe benefits further the purposes of the exempt organization.

3. If a minister's total compensation is less than $100,000, the board should decide which survey or set of surveys, both nonprofit and for profit, it will use to determine salary and benefits. If total compensation exceeds $100,000, careful consideration should be given to retaining a recognized compensation consultant to conduct a study the board can use in its deliberations.

4. Keep a logbook or record showing the specific business purpose of each use of company autos or church credit cards.

5. Competent tax counsel should be retained if significant areas exist that might give rise to other penalties, such as "closing agreement" fines, under prior IRS practice. It is likely that the IRS will continue using closing agreements to reach "private benefit" transactions that it cannot touch under the new law (for example, executive recruitment incentives, or payments to an individual who cannot influence the charity, and so is not considered a "disqualified person." Other examples might be substantial sales of church assets to non-insiders, and payments for outside fund-raisers).

6. Revenue sharing and incentive compensation arrangements should be carefully examined to be sure they do not violate the new law. In the past, the IRS has taken the position that any revenue-sharing arrangement is inurement per se, and that they are prohibited even if they result in reasonable compensation. But in other cases, the IRS has used a "cost benefit analysis" to allow some types of incentive compensation, but not others. For example, so-called "net-revenue sharing" is mostly forbidden, but arrangements in which gross revenues are the basis for a percentage split have been permitted if a "real discernible business purpose" was found for the arrangement. The new law was apparently intended to penalize "revenue stream transactions," but broad-based employee incentive compensation plans would be approved. Unfortunately, the Committee Report does not specifically explain how revenue splits can be accomplished, although the legislative history of the Act cites only IRS General Counsel Memoranda in which incentive compensation arrangements were approved and percentage compensation was found not to constitute private inurement. The House Report also contains a statement that Treasury and the IRS are not bound by previous general counsel memoranda if they write regulations for the new law. Churches need to file comments with the IRS about how these kinds of arrangements should work for ministers, and how they promulgate theological beliefs, such as "living by faith."

7. Miscellaneous benefits may be subject to the new penalty tax unless meticulous documentation and analysis is followed.

8. Audit current taxable types of fringe benefits to ensure they are reported as wages on the individual's W-2, 1099 and/or 990.

9. Determine whether the church will provide reimbursement to its minister(s) if the IRS assesses the new penalty tax against them. In addition, review church insurance (liability and D&O coverage) policies to determine if a rider can be added that will insure against such penalty

taxes. It is important to document reimbursements and/or premium payments as included in the individual's compensation package. The board should also decide whether reimbursements will be paid to, or for, ministers who are no longer on staff at the church. The board might consider an agreement in which reimbursement would be paid if the minister agreed to repay the excess benefits to the church (because this could avoid the 200 percent penalty).

10.   Consider applying the following:

    a.   Written employment agreements;

    b.   Annual performance evaluations using objective criteria;

    c.   A conflict of interest policy, for noncompensatory transactions with disqualified persons;

    d.   A procedure for monitoring compliance;

    e.   List who may be subject to the tax (disqualified persons); and

    f.   Look at transactions with disqualified persons.

Appendix 10
New IRS Regulations

As outlined in appendix 9, section 4958 was enacted in section 1311 of the Taxpayer Bill of Rights 2. Section 4958 applies to a minister's salary on or after September 14, 1995. Section 4958 imposes penalty taxes where the IRS thinks a minister is receiving excess benefits. The IRS has just released proposed regulations relating to how the new penalty taxes will work.

Here are some of the highlights from the new regulations:

- The safe harbor will apply when a church board approves general guidelines for entering into transactions with ministers generally, rather than voting on each individual transaction.
- The safe harbor will apply when salary approval is given by a church compensation committee that is not composed exclusively of church directors or trustees.
- The church board or committee will be considered independent if members recuse themselves when they have conflicts of interest.
- The regulations allow a church's board to delegate the responsibility for setting compensation to an independent committee (this is a key point for churches).
- The regulations clarify that no negative inference should be drawn if a church does not avail itself of the safe harbor.
- The regulations clarify that compensation outside the range of comparables is not per se unreasonable.
- Some church representatives (including your author) submitted comments noting that the religious beliefs of some churches and some state laws regarding churches prevent churches from benefiting from the rebuttable presumption of reasonableness because of the identity of the parties required to approve compensation arrangements or other transactions. While the new regulations do not provide a special exception for churches from the requirements that must be met to give rise to the safe harbor, they do provide churches with a special rule stating that the procedures of section 7611 will be used in initiating and conducting any inquiry or examination into whether an excess benefit transaction has occurred between a church and a minister. (Section 7611 is the special code section giving churches unique safeguards against IRS audits.) For purposes of this rule, the reasonable belief required to initiate a church tax inquiry is satisfied if there is a reasonable belief that a section 4958 tax is due from a disqualified person with respect to a transaction involving a church.

How Churches Can Qualify for the Safe Harbor

The proposed regulations provide that a compensation arrangement between a church and a minister is presumed to be reasonable, and a transfer of property, a right to use property, or any other benefit or privilege between a church and a minister is presumed to be at fair market value, if three conditions are satisfied.

The three conditions are as follows:

1. The compensation arrangement or terms of transfer are approved by the church's governing body or a committee of the governing body composed entirely of individuals who do not have a conflict of interest with respect to the arrangement or transaction;

2. The governing body, or committee thereof, obtained and relied upon appropriate data as to comparability prior to making its determination; and
3. The governing body or committee adequately documented the basis for its determination concurrently with making that determination.

The safe harbor established by satisfying these three requirements may be rebutted by additional information showing that the compensation was not reasonable or that the transfer was not at fair market value. However, the likelihood of such a rebuttal is likely to be remote in most transactions involving churches.

To the extent permitted under local law, the governing body of a church may authorize other parties to act on its behalf by following specified procedures that satisfy the three requirements for invoking the safe harbor. An arrangement or transaction that is subsequently approved by the board's designee or designees in accordance with those procedures will be subject to the safe harbor even though the governing body does not vote separately on the specific arrangement or transaction.

With respect to the first requirement, the proposed regulations provide that the governing body is the board of directors, board of trustees or equivalent controlling body of the church.

A committee of the governing body may be composed of any individuals permitted under state law to serve on such a committee, and may act on behalf of the governing body to the extent permitted by state law.

The proposed regulations provide that a member of the governing body, or committee thereof, does not have a conflict of interest with respect to a compensation arrangement or transaction if the member is not the minister involved and is not related to the minister participating in or economically benefiting from the compensation arrangement or transaction; is not in an employment relationship subject to the direction or control of the minister participating in or economically benefiting from the compensation arrangement or transaction; is not receiving compensation or other payments subject to approval by the minister participating in or economically benefiting from the compensation arrangement or transaction; has no material financial interest affected by the compensation arrangement or transaction; and does not approve a transaction providing economic benefits to any minister participating in the compensation arrangement or transaction, who in turn has approved or will approve a transaction providing economic benefits to the member.

An arrangement or transaction has not been approved by a committee of a governing body if, under the governing documents of the church or state law, the committee's decision must be ratified by the full governing body in order to become effective.

With respect to the second requirement for the rebuttable presumption of reasonableness, the proposed regulations provide that a governing body or committee has appropriate data on comparability if, given the knowledge and expertise of its members, it has information sufficient to determine whether a compensation arrangement will result in the payment of reasonable compensation or a transaction will be for fair market value.

Relevant information includes, but is not limited to, compensation levels paid by similarly situated churches (as well as other organizations, both taxable and tax-exempt) for functionally comparable positions; the availability of similar services in the geographic area of the church; independent compensation surveys compiled by independent firms; actual written offers from similar churches competing for the services of the minister; and independent appraisals of the value of property that the church intends to purchase from, or sell or provide to the minister.

A special rule is provided for churches with annual gross receipts of less than $1 million. Under this rule, when the governing body reviews compensation arrangements, it will be considered to have appropriate data as to comparability if it has data on compensation paid by five comparable churches in the same or similar communities for similar services. No inference is intended with respect to whether circumstances failing outside this safe harbor will meet the requirements with respect to the collection of appropriate data.

For purposes of the third requirement of the safe harbor under the proposed regulations, to be documented adequately, the written or electronic records of the governing body or committee must note:

- The terms of the transaction that was approved
- The date it was approved
- The members of the governing body or committee who were present during debate on the transaction or arrangement that was approved
- Those members who voted on it
- The comparability data obtained and relied upon by the committee
- How the data was obtained
- The actions taken with respect to consideration of the transaction by anyone who is otherwise a member of the governing body or committee but who had a conflict of interest with respect to the transaction or arrangement
- If the governing body or committee determines that reasonable compensation for a specific arrangement or fair market value in a specific transaction is higher or lower than the range of comparable data obtained, the governing body or committee must record the basis for its determination
- For a decision to be documented concurrently, records must be prepared by the next meeting of the governing body or committee occurring after the final action or actions of the governing body or committee are taken
- Records must be reviewed and approved by the governing body or committee as reasonable, accurate and complete within a reasonable time period thereafter.

Advice of Counsel Exception

If a person, after full disclosure of the factual situation to legal counsel (including in-house counsel) relies on the advice of such counsel expressed in a reasoned written legal opinion that a transaction is not an excess benefit transaction, the person's participation in such transaction will ordinarily not be considered knowing or willful and will ordinarily be considered due to reasonable cause, even if the transaction is later held to be an excess benefit transaction.

Family Members of Ministers

A person is a disqualified person with respect to any transaction with a church if the person is a member of the family of a minister whose salary is being determined in any transaction with the same church. A minister's family is considered to include:

(i)	Spouse
(ii)	Brothers or sisters (by whole or half blood)
(iii)	Spouses of brothers or sisters (by whole or half blood)
(iv)	Ancestors
(v)	Children
(vi)	Grandchildren
(vii)	Great grandchildren and
(viii)	Spouses of children, grandchildren and great grandchildren.

Actual Language from the New Regulations

Following are some selected passages from the new regulations of particular interest to churches and ministers:

Compensation for purposes of section 4958 includes all items of compensation provided by a [church] in exchange for the performance of services. These items of compensation include, but are not limited to:

(A)   All forms of cash and noncash compensation, including salary, fees, bonuses, and severance payments paid;

(B)   All forms of deferred compensation that is earned and vested, whether or not funded, and whether or not paid under a deferred compensation plan that is a qualified plan under section 401 (a), but if deferred compensation for services performed in multiple prior years vests in a later year, then that compensation is attributed to the years in which the services were performed;

(C)   The amount of premiums paid for liability or any other insurance coverage, as well as any payment or reimbursement by the [church] of charges, expenses, fees, or taxes not covered ultimately by the insurance coverage;

(D)   All other benefits, whether or not included in income for tax purposes, including payments to welfare benefit plans on behalf of the persons being compensated, such as plans providing medical, dental, life insurance, severance pay, and disability benefits, and both taxable and nontaxable fringe benefits [other than working condition fringe benefits described in section 132(d) and *de minimis* fringe benefits described in section 132(e)], including expense allowances or reimbursements or foregone interest on loans that the recipient must report as income on his separate income tax return; and

(E)   Any economic benefit provided by a [church], whether provided directly or through another entity owned, controlled by or affiliated with the [church], whether such other entity is taxable or tax-exempt.

W.4958-6 *Rebuttable presumption that transaction is not an excess benefit transaction.*

(a)   *In general.* Payments under a compensation arrangement between a [church] and a disqualified person shall be presumed to be reasonable, and a transfer of property, right to use property, or any other benefit or privilege between a [church] and a disqualified person shall be presumed to be at fair market value, if the following conditions are satisfied:

   (1)   The compensation arrangement or terms of transfer are approved by the organization's governing body or a committee of the governing body composed entirely of individuals who do not have a conflict of interest with respect to the arrangement or transaction;

   (2)   The governing body, or committee thereof, obtained and relied upon appropriate data as to comparability prior to making its determination; and

   (3)   The governing body or committee adequately documented the basis for its determination concurrently with making that determination.

(b)   *Delegation pursuant to procedures.* To the extent permitted under local law, the governing body of a [church] may authorize other parties to act on its behalf by following specified procedures that satisfy the three requirements for invoking the rebuttable presumption of reasonableness. An arrangement or transaction that is subsequently approved by the board's designee or designees in accordance with those procedures shall be subject to the rebuttable presumption even though the governing body does not vote separately on the specific arrangement or transaction.

(c)   *Rebutting the Presumption.* The presumption established by satisfying the three requirements of paragraph (a) of this section may be rebutted by additional information showing that the compensation was not reasonable or that the transfer was not at fair market value.

(d)   *Requirements for invoking rebuttable presumption—*

   (1)   *Disinterested governing body or committee—*

      (i)   *In general.* The governing body is the board of directors, board of trustees, or equivalent controlling body of the [church]. A committee of the governing body may be composed of any individuals permitted under state law to serve on such a committee, and may act on behalf of the governing body to the extent permitted by state law. However, if the rebuttable presumption arises as the result of actions taken by a committee, any members of such a committee who are not members of the governing body are deemed to be organization managers for purposes of the tax imposed by section 4958(a)(2), subject to the rules of ß53.4958-1(d).

(ii) *Persons not included on governing body or committee.* For purposes of determining whether the requirements of paragraph (a) of this section have been met with respect to a specific transaction or compensation arrangement, a person is not included on the governing body or committee when it is reviewing a transaction if that person meets with other members only to answer questions, and otherwise recuses himself from the meeting and is not present during debate and voting on the transaction or compensation arrangement.

(iii) *Absence of conflict of interest.* A member of the governing body, or committee thereof, does not have a conflict of interest with respect to a compensation arrangement or transaction if the member:

  (A) Is not the disqualified person and is not related to any disqualified person participating in or economically benefiting from the compensation arrangement or transaction by a relationship described in section 4958(f)(4) or ß53.4958-3(b)(1);

  (B) Is not in an employment relationship subject to the direction or control of any disqualified person participating in or economically benefiting from the compensation arrangement or transaction;

  (C) Is not receiving compensation or other payments subject to approval by any disqualified person participating in or economically benefiting from the compensation arrangement or transaction;

  (D) Has no material financial interest affected by the compensation arrangement or transaction; and

  (E) Does not approve a transaction providing economic benefits to any disqualified person participating in the compensation arrangement or transaction, who in turn has approved or will approve a transaction providing economic benefits to the member.

(iv) *Rule where ratification by full governing body required.* An arrangement or transaction has not been approved by a committee of a governing body if, under the governing documents of the organization or state law, the committee's decision must be ratified by the full governing body in order to become effective.

(2) *Appropriate data as to comparability—*

  (i) *In general.* A governing body or committee has appropriate data as to comparability if, given the knowledge and expertise of its members, it has information sufficient to determine whether, under the standards set forth in ß 53.4958-4(b), a compensation arrangement will result in the payment of reasonable compensation or a transaction will be for fair market value. Relevant information would include, but not be limited to, compensation levels paid by similarly situated organizations, both taxable and tax-exempt, for functionally comparable positions; the availability of similar services in the geographic area of the applicable tax-exempt organization; independent compensation surveys compiled by independent firms; actual written offers from similar institutions competing for the services of the disqualified person; and independent appraisals of the value of property that the applicable organization intends to purchase from, or sell or provide to, the disqualified person.

  (ii) *Special rule for compensation paid by small organizations.* For organizations with annual gross receipts of less than $1 million reviewing compensation arrangements, the governing body or committee will be considered to have appropriate data as to comparability if it has data on compensation paid by five comparable organizations in the same or similar communities for similar services. No inference is intended with respect to whether circumstances failing outside this safe harbor will meet the requirement with respect to the collection of appropriate data.

    (iii) *Additional rules for special rule for small organizations.* For purposes of determining applicability of the special rule for small organizations described in paragraph (d)(2)(ii) of this section, a rolling average based on the three prior taxable years may be used to calculate annual gross receipts of an organization. If any applicable tax-exempt organization is affiliated with another entity by common control or governing documents, the annual gross receipts of all such related organizations must be aggregated to determine applicability of the special rule stated in paragraph (d)(2)(ii) of this section.

(3) *Documentation—*

    (i) For a decision to be documented adequately, the written or electronic records of the governing body or committee must note:

        (A) The terms of the transaction that was approved and the date it was approved;

        (B) The members of the governing body or committee who were present during debate on the transaction or arrangement that was approved and those who voted on it;

        (C) The comparability data obtained and relied upon by the committee and how the data was obtained; and

        (D) The actions taken with respect to consideration of the transaction by anyone who is otherwise a member of the governing body or committee but who had a conflict of interest with respect to the transaction or arrangement.

    (ii) If the governing body or committee determines that reasonable compensation for a specific arrangement or fair market value in a specific transaction is higher or lower than the range of comparable data obtained, the governing body or committee must record the basis for its determination. For a decision to be documented concurrently, records must be prepared by the next meeting of the governing body or committee occurring after the final action or actions of the governing body or committee are taken. Records must be reviewed and approved by the governing body or committee as reasonable, accurate and complete within a reasonable time period thereafter.

(e) *No presumption until circumstances exist to determine reasonableness of compensation.* If reasonableness of the compensation cannot be determined based on circumstances existing at the date when a contract for services was made, then the rebuttable presumption of this section cannot arise until circumstances exist so that reasonableness of compensation can be determined, and the three requirements for the presumption under paragraph (d) of this section subsequently are satisfied.

(f) *No inference from absence of presumption.* The fact that a transaction between a [church] and a disqualified person is not subject to the presumption described in this section shall not create any inference that the transaction is an excess benefit transaction. Neither shall the fact that a transaction qualifies for the presumption exempt or relieve any person from compliance with any federal or state law imposing any obligation, duty, responsibility, or other standard of conduct with respect to the operation or administration of any [church].

(g) *Period of reliance on rebuttable presumption.* The rebuttable presumption applies to all payments made or transactions completed in accordance with a contract provided that the three requirements of the rebuttable presumption were met at the time the contract was agreed upon.

W.4958-7 *Special rules.*

(b) *Interaction between section 4958 and section 7611 rules for church tax inquiries and examinations.* The procedures of section 7611 will be used in initiating and conducting any inquiry or examination into whether an excess benefit transaction has occurred between a church and a disqualified person. For purposes of this rule, the reasonable belief required to initiate a church tax inquiry is satisfied if there is a reasonable belief that a section 4958 tax is due from a disqualified person with respect to a transaction involving a church. See §301.7611-1 Q&A 19 of this chapter. §53.4963-1 [Amended].

Par. 9. In §301.7611-1, the Table of Contents is amended by adding "Application to Section 4958 19" immediately after "Effective Date 18."

Par. 10. In §301.7611-1, an undesignated center heading and Q-19 and A-19 are added to read as follows:

4301.7611-1 *Questions and answers relating to church tax inquiries and examinations.*

Application to Section 4958

Q-19: When do the church tax inquiry and examination procedures described in section 7611 apply to a determination of whether there was an excess benefit transaction described in section 4958?

A-19: See §53.4958-7(b) of this chapter for rules governing the interaction between section 4958 excise taxes on excess benefit transactions and section 7611 church tax inquiry and examination procedures.

This ClergyTax® book discusses a wide range of legal and tax issues of concern to ministers and churches, but it is not a substitute for legal advice.

Appendix 11
New Laws and Rules That Affect Ministers and Churches

Congress has added more new rules which affect ministers and churches. Fortunately, the news is not all bad. Here are some of the more important rules ministers need to be familiar with:

1. Since January 1, 1997, churches have been allowed to have so-called 401(k) retirement plans. These are the standard corporate type retirement plans. Two cautions for now: (i) startup costs can be high for these plans; and (ii) the new law omitted any mention of allowing 403(b) plans to rollover assets into a newly created 401(k) plan; this means churches that set up a 401(k) plan under the new law would also have to maintain their 403(b) plans, so the church would end up with recordkeeping for two retirement plans.

2. You've probably heard of "subchapter S" corporations. Now, churches (and some church pension plans also) can be shareholders in these kinds of corporations. But there is a drawback: income flowing to the church from the sub-S will be considered taxable to the church, and the church will have to file Form 990-T to report it (Form 990 is the form the IRS uses to select non-profit corporations for audit).

3. Ministers' professional associations may now dispense with the rule that made membership fees non-deductible to the minister if they were used for political purposes, and the organization can pay the "section 527 tax" instead. However, membership fees used for lobbying expenses will still be non-deductible to member ministers.

4. Churches can now band together and form their own insurance companies, called "charitable risk pools". These pools can buy mass policies on a reduced premium basis from established carriers. This new type of pool will be tax exempt under Code Section 501(n).

5. Nonprofit organizations that lobby Congress, but do not spend more than $20,000 in total lobbying expenses during a six-month period, do not have to register under the Lobbying Disclosure Act. Also, "grassroots lobbying" is excluded from the definition of lobbying. Grassroots lobbying occurs when a nonprofit organization encourages the general public to lobby. This can be done by means of television or written means, where the organization urges the public to contact Congress on a matter. Nonprofit organizations can also engage freely in "self-defense" lobbying, which means lobbying about laws which might affect the existence of the organization, its powers and duties, tax-exempt status, or the deduction of contributions to the organization.

6. Retired ministers may now receive a housing allowance, and owe no Social Security tax on it. Utilities are also covered. This benefit is retroactive, and retired ministers who paid Social Security tax on their housing allowances in 1996, 1997 or 1998 can file amended returns to claim a refund. Retired ministers should check this information carefully, because potential refunds for each year can run into the thousands of dollars.

7. Since January 1, 1997, self-employed ministers have been allowed to deduct contributions made to church pension plans. I had published this advice for several years, based on my review of published IRS rulings. However, recently the IRS had disagreed, saying self-employed ministers could participate in, but not deduct contributions to, church pension plans. Now Congress has settled the issue once and for all.

8. If your church has more than 50 employees, you should check with the insurance company that provides your group health plan. There are new rules for portability, pre-existing conditions, exclusions from coverage, and guaranteed renewability. These new rules do not apply to churches that don't have more than 50 employees as long as any rule violations are the fault of their insurance provider.

9. Depending on their income, ministers may be able to claim up to a $400 credit for each qualifying child under age 17. New this year, the child tax credit could reduce the tax to zero, or even become a refundable credit for ministers with three or more qualifying children.

10. Ministers can benefit from a number of educational incentives. The Hope credit lets ministers below certain income levels claim a credit for the first two years of post-secondary education. It's limited to $1,500 per year for qualified tuition and expenses. The lifetime learning credit applies to qualified tuition and expenses for undergraduate, graduate and professional degree courses paid after June 30, 1998, for courses starting after that date. The credit is 20 percent of expenses, up to $1,000 per return. Certain limits apply to both credits.

11. In addition to these credits, ministers can set up Education IRAs featuring nondeductible contributions of up to $500 a year for a named beneficiary under age 18. And ministers can tap into their other IRAs to pay for qualified higher education expenses. Also, a limited amount of interest paid on higher education loans is deductible. Some restrictions apply to each benefit.

12. Another new IRA is the Roth IRA. It features nondeductible contributions, with tax-free distributions if they begin after the fifth year the minister has a Roth IRA, the minister is at least age 59 or disabled, or the distribution is a qualified first-time home buyer distribution.

13. New capital gains tax rules may reduce the tax owed on investments. The benefits of lower rates now apply to sales of property held more than one year instead of 18 months. Schedule D will take ministers step by step through the rates and rules.

14. The earned income tax credit (EITC) could be worth a few dollars, or up to $3,816 for ministers with more than one qualifying child, up to $2,312 for one qualifying child. For those with no children, the EITC could be worth up to $347. The amount ministers can earn and still be eligible for the credit in 1999 is $30,580 for those with more than one child, $26,928 with one qualifying child, and $10,200 with no children.

15. Rules for getting installment agreements, offers in compromise and innocent spouse relief are now less stringent. And ministers who haven't been able to resolve their problems through normal IRS channels have a new toll-free line to a taxpayer advocate: 1-877-777- 4778.

16. Social Security numbers will not be printed anywhere on the tax instruction booklets or labels, so ministers need to make sure they put their correct SSNs on their tax returns and other forms. And those who owe taxes can write their checks to the United States Treasury, but don't staple the check to the return.

17. Get details on these topics and more in the tax instruction booklets or in free IRS Publication 553, *Highlights of 1999 Tax Changes*. Call 1-800-829-3676 to order. Or check out the IRS Web site at www.irs.ustreas.gov. (Be sure to set your web browser on "stun.")